"From afar, I was getting the 'I'm Ok' pings from the GPS locator she carried on her hikes. Little did I understand the strenuous journey of discernment that was also unfolding as Diane carried these beautiful families' stories in her heart. My hope is that the principles of the ten cairns will be a beacon of hope for those on whatever journey they are on."
   — **Matt D. Whaley,** Market Director, SCI Colorado Funeral Services

"An exquisite collection of spirit-full insights garnered during her many days on foot in wild places. The ten 'cairns' or 'waypoints' for living that she realizes along the way will serve all of us on our journeys, no matter what path we walk."
   — **Rick Kempa,** editor, Deep Wild Journal

"Parallel to her physical journey, Diane shares her profound experiences as a life-cycle celebrant. These two paths converge beautifully, as Diane discovers deep connections between her trail experiences and the lives she honors. Through vivid descriptions of both inner and outer landscapes, she offers readers a source of inspiration and strength for their own personal journeys."
   — **Ben Martin,** Executive Director of Natural Transitions Institute, poet, and past Chairman of the Board for The Celebrant Foundation & Institute

"Diane's journey reminds us that humanness is not something we experience in isolation, but when we are in community together. This book brings that understanding front and center and along the way brings us all a little closer to experience our full humanity. Her journey along the Continental Divide Trail takes us through some of the most awe-inspiring landscapes and places not just in North America, but the whole planet."
   — **Teresa Martinez,** Executive Director, Continental Divide Trail Coalition

THE WAYPOINTS

THE WAYPOINTS

FROM 400 FAREWELLS AND 3,000 MILES

DIANE "GRACE" GANSAUER

Interfaith Minister, Master Celebrant,
Hiker on the Continental Divide

Lyrical Life Press   Evergreen, Colorado

LyricalLifeCeremonies.com | CeremoniesDiane@gmail.com

The Waypoints: From 400 Farewells and 3,000 Miles

ISBN 979-8-9922211-1-4 (paperback)
ISBN 979-8-9922211-0-7 (eBook)
Library of Congress Control Number: 2025902168

Publication managed by AuthorImprints.com

This book is intended to provide accurate information with regard to its subject matter and reflects the opinion and perspective of the author. However, in times of rapid change, ensuring all information provided is entirely accurate and up-to-date at all times is not always possible. Therefore, the author and publisher accept no responsibility for inaccuracies or omissions and specifically disclaim any liability, loss, or risk, personal, professional, or otherwise, which may be incurred as a consequence, directly or indirectly, of the use and/or application of any of the contents of this book.

This book is dedicated to all the families I have had
the honor of companioning in their journey of grief.

I also dedicate this book to those who were my companions
in my journey along the Continental Divide.

And finally, I wish to honor the historical ownership of the
land that I crossed. Much, if not all, of the land that the
Continental Divide Trail (the CDT) passes through was
taken from Native American ownership. I walked across
land that originally belonged to at least eighteen tribes.

The finite manifests the infinite.
  • *Francis of Assisi, as interpreted by Richard Rohr*

TABLE OF CONTENTS

INTRODUCTION

Why I Wrote This Book

This is not a book about grief. Nor is it a hiking journal. Instead, it's about "walking home" to your best self. It's about the stories we are remembered by and the legacy we leave. And it's about falling in love with life again—well past what American culture considers to be our prime years.

I was in my fifties when I took up hiking again—something I hadn't done since I was in my teens. I looked at my life as an empty nester and decided to hike the Colorado Trail. That was the beginning of a new chapter in my life.

The Colorado Trail stretches 567* miles from Denver to the southwest corner of the state. Due to my full-time work

---

* 567 miles is the total length of the Colorado Trail including both alternative routes through the Collegiate Mountains; I hiked both routes. The spectacular section through the western Collegiates, which overlaps with the CDT, inspired me to complete the trek from Mexico to Canada along the Continental Divide.

schedule, I hiked one section at a time, almost exclusively in the summer. I became enthralled by nature's wonders on the trail, and especially the mountains where this trail overlapped the Continental Divide.

In 2016, at age sixty-one, I was eager to kick it up a notch by expanding my hikes beyond Colorado. At least, that's what I told my husband, who knew better than to warn me off. I'm glad he didn't. I committed to hiking the entire length of the Continental Divide Trail (the CDT), from the US border with Mexico to the US border with Canada.

By that time, I had officiated 180 celebrations of life—memorial services, funerals, and gatherings focused on honoring the lives of individuals I became acquainted with in detail after they had passed away. By the time I finished all thirty-one hundred miles of the CDT, I had officiated more than four hundred memorial services and funerals. And my time on the trail was transcendent.

More than a century earlier, my ancestors walked from the middle of the country to the West Coast on the Oregon Trail while others headed west for the rush on precious metals and borax in Death Valley. It felt like this long walk I set out to complete was part of my identity. But as I embarked, this pursuit was secondary to my work-life and priorities at home. I didn't foresee how it would consume me. I underestimated the powerful dose of resilience we get from putting our feet on the dirt and challenging our physical limits. And I had no idea how transformative extended time in nature can be in connecting us with the rich goodness of life from an ancient perspective.

My brother and frequent hiking partner often said, "The trail will do its work on us." He was right. A landscape that lasts millennia shakes mere mortals down to the essentials. As a woman who had entered my sixties by the time I turned my attention to the Continental Divide, hiking grounded me in a pared-down perspective on what is good, necessary, and stands the test of time.

Who knew whether I would be able to embrace a new chapter in my life as I entered my senior years? And who knew how much time I had left? While this long hike required adjustment for the abilities and comforts of an older body, this multiyear effort resulted in far more than it might have years earlier. It offered profound reflection on the qualities that matter in life, and even in the legacy we leave.

Most of all, this experience over seven years gave me a deeper appreciation of the lives of more than four hundred people I'd never met. It opened me to learn from them.

In 2012, I was certified by the Celebrant Foundation to prepare ceremonies across the life cycle and immediately began assisting families with funerals. I have always enjoyed creative collaborations and exploring the link between creativity and spirituality. Being a celebrant brought this back into the forefront in my life.

As a funeral celebrant, I accompany families through the beginning of their grief journey, when the loss of a loved one is raw. After extensive interviews, each life consumes my thoughts. I consider how to shape a person's experiences into a story that helps their families to honor them in their hearts and minds forever.

This has given me an intensely personal view of the richness of life. Indeed, honoring lives has renewed my *appreciation* for life. All lives are a mixture of joy and suffering, often with a dash of questionable choices blending with a sprinkle of wisdom. My ceremonies are expressions of faith that each life contains goodness. No matter how much darkness there may be, families and I find the spark of light that people we love have left behind.

Hiking the CDT added a new layer of perspective to this work. Extremely long hikes combined with memorializing the goodness in the lives I had encountered created a second wave of energy and purpose in my autumn years. I began to see our life stories in the context of both their grittiness and the renewal of nature.

Lessons while hiking along the spine of the continent overlapped with the stacked stones of life stories that burrowed deep within me. Those stories stirred with the dust and sweat of mile after mile of walking through wild places. New insights rose like monuments along the trail. After long hours of solo reflections, I was inspired to write down what I was learning.

By the time I completed the CDT on August 28, 2023, I was sixty-seven years old. I was transformed by pursuing what I had fallen in love with—the sacredness all around me, in nature and in lives. My purpose became to share these insights.

How I Wrote This Book

Because themes and connecting insights don't come together on a predictable timeline, this book is organized thematically rather than chronologically. However, it generally follows my northbound progress from Mexico to Canada.

To start writing, I charted the most salient experiences on the trail and noted several themes. Then I reread every ceremony I'd written over the course of nine years. The significant overlapping insights from the trail and the life stories entrusted to me became the waypoints in this book. These jumped out as guideposts for life as well as being pertinent to the iconic walk from border to border.

Next, I selected specific life stories. With the permission of my former boss, the market director of the funeral homes, I began contacting families. In many cases, I had been out of touch with the family for several years. The warmth they offered was overwhelming, as was their trust and permission to publish their stories. While most of the names are true, the few exceptions are from families I was unable to reach. In those cases, I changed identifying details but kept the message intact. My goal is to honor all these loved ones in a deep and authentic manner by connecting them to a timeless perspective.

The landscape outlasts us all. Highlighting threads of nature's lessons interwoven with those of everyday life stories affords us the opportunity to contemplate what really matters over time. These are also the qualities that people who love us are most likely to cherish after we are gone.

The waypoints that follow signify guidelines for a good life. May they inspire us all.

How to Enjoy This Book

To set the scene for the stories, I have provided a map of the CDT and a summary of how I managed this adventure. I also define key words and why they are important.

In each waypoint section:

- *The trail introduces the thematic material of the waypoint.*

- *I share stories about people whose lives and the ceremonies honoring them reflect the waypoint. Each story begins with the individual's name and the length of their life.*
- *I close with trail stories that connect the life stories to nature's timeless wisdom.*

Each section ends with a few questions for the reader to consider. They may be useful for journaling, for discussion with family, or discussing with friends in a book club. If you wish to move on to more stories rather than pause to reflect on the questions, please do. Perhaps you will return to them later. The path is yours to choose.

THE CONTINENTAL DIVIDE NATIONAL SCENIC TRAIL

The Continental Divide National Scenic Trail (the CDT) spans thirty-one hundred miles from the US border with Mexico to the US border with Canada. It crosses New Mexico, Colorado, Wyoming, part of the Idaho border, and Montana.

How I hiked this trail: The overall project initially appeared insurmountable. Seeing CDT hikers on the trail with huge backpacks, I used to say, "I will never do that!" One should be careful with the word "never." After studying paper maps and a popular hiker app, I broke down the thirty-one hundred miles into feasible pieces. I walked eleven hundred miles alone, one-thousand miles with my oldest brother, and one-thousand miles with other hiking partners—almost all of this after I turned sixty.

After completing the Colorado portion of the CDT on the Colorado Trail, I began marching north from New Mexico in

April of 2017 at the age of sixty-one. I was what hikers call a LASH—long-a**-section-hiker—completing the trail one piece at a time. I spent several months training and planning logistics each year and only hiked the CDT in spring and summer in order to avoid snow in the mountains.

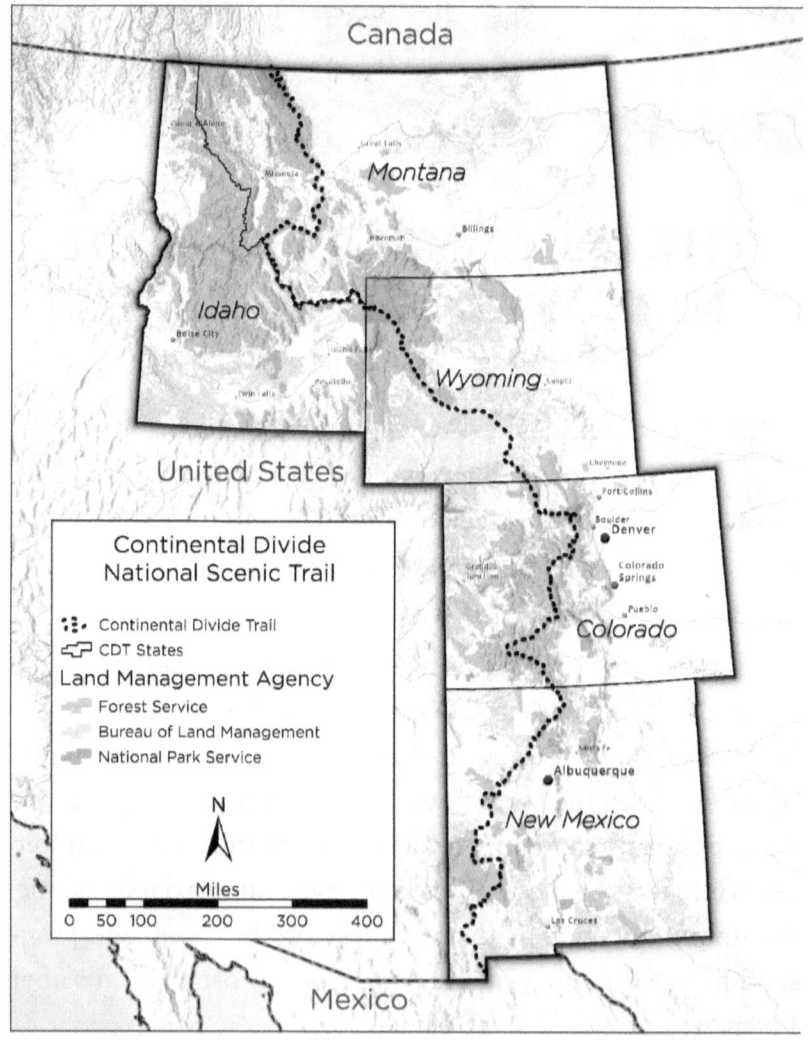

My hikes averaged fifteen miles per day, but not always in a sequence; I picked sections each year according to weather, snow on the ground, best dates to find water, the presence of other hikers (preferably), and transportation. I usually needed to be dropped off at one end of a section and have either my car or an arranged ride at the other end. I avoided hitchhiking. "Sections" were around one hundred miles initially but grew to more than five hundred miles in the summers of 2021 and 2022.

Every four or five days, I usually went into a town to resupply food at a store or via a box I'd mailed to a hostel; I could also take a shower, get rid of trash, and sleep in a bed.

The CDT is renowned for long stretches that are quite remote. When I couldn't carry enough food between towns, I paid someone to deliver food to me by four-wheel drive vehicle, by hiking in, or on horseback. If I wasn't in a federally designated wilderness or national park, my provisions could be hidden in bear-proof cannisters that I paid someone to hide off the trail. I used this option only once and retrieved the used cannisters afterward via the nearest road.

"Insurmountable" became "feasible." I completed the thirty-one hundred miles of the Continental Divide Trail, crossing into Canada accompanied by family on August 28, 2023, when I was sixty-seven.

THE WAYPOINTS

This book shares the waypoints that emerged from life stories and experiences in nature like stone markers on a trail—guideposts on the path to a good life.

A ccording to Merriam-Webster.com, a waypoint is "an intermediate point on a route or line of travel." It is a term familiar to hikers on long trails, where they must regularly confirm they are going in the right direction. Waypoints might be marked on a map; they could include trail junctions or other significant features in the landscape. On life's path, aren't we *all* looking for waypoints to confirm we're heading in the right direction?

Sometimes in the mountains, where the soil is so thin that it disappears and only rocks remain, with nary a directional sign in sight, then a waypoint might be marked by a cairn, "a heap of stones piled up as a landmark or memorial" (also defined by Merriam-Webster.com). The dictionary intelligentsia say its pronounced "kern," but all my hiker friends pronounce it "kayrn." Some public land managers discourage modifying the land by building cairns; nonetheless, they are common in several sections of the CDT.

Where a trail's direction might be confusing, hikers often assemble cairns as directional guides. It's common for stones to be added to them over many years. In a stark way, they are beautiful. I fell in love with them. I was especially relieved to see a cairn on the horizon when I was in a lonely place and uncertain which way to go.

Waypoints might be on a map or a navigation app, but cairns are *physical* waypoints, created by the trail community to help people who come down the trail. They can be critical notifications for hikers to proceed safely. And they boost the confidence of those continuing on their intended path.

Cairns are also familiar to people with Celtic heritage (including me). In Ireland and Scotland, cairns memorialize people of significance.

Over my many years on the CDT, as I pondered the life stories I encountered during the period when my hikes stretched across the continent, the cairns took on this other definition: a memorial. They reminded me of lives that pointed to the best way to go.

Consider with me the waypoints of both resilient sources: the trail and remarkable lives.

Each waypoint in this book is introduced with a photo of a cairn that I passed while walking the Continental Divide.

WALK TOWARD
WHAT SUSTAINS YOU

On the second day of hiking in the Chihuahuan Desert of New Mexico, one of my hiking partners became so dehydrated that both her speech and walk meandered. She had been drinking far less than her body needed for hiking in a hot, parched landscape. Our team of three quickly reduced to two when we got her off the trail so she could recover. It was the middle of April in 2017. I was at the US border with Mexico beginning my hike on the Continental Divide Trail (the CDT) to Canada. Right away, I was occupied with finding water.

That quest for precious, essential, life-nurturing water continued for the rest of the hike to our country's northern border, thirty-one hundred miles away. More than that, it also became a metaphor for a critical lesson from the life stories I carried: Moving forward successfully requires actively seeking out what is vital.

As a professional celebrant, I lead ceremonies that center on the stories behind life's significant transitions. As I uncover the life story of someone who has passed away, a stranger becomes someone whom I help a family to honor in an authentic and meaningful way.

The essence of each life story is this: What principles did this person build their life on? What did they value? What kind of person did they become? How will they be remembered?

It didn't matter whether the families I interviewed were wealthy or of modest means, or had a specific ethnic, racial, cultural or spiritual background. The families commonly defined the essence of a good life in this way: a life of good character, a life of enduring love, a life that found light in times of darkness, a life that demonstrated vision and hope for the future, and a life that expressed gratitude for grace along life's path.

Seeking the wellspring of what is vital to surviving a very long and difficult journey, or the wellspring to being our best self in the time we're given, could make the difference between being strong for the duration or wandering off into oblivion. In the hundreds of lives I observed, clear intent to pursue what mattered meant the difference between a full life that energized and inspired, versus a directionless meander that left little behind.

Families' insights into what counts as a worthwhile life frequently overlapped with what I was learning in the deserts and mountains along America's Continental Divide.

Charlie, fifty-two years

Specific qualities of character consistently inspire families when considering a loved one who is held in high regard. Among the hundreds of family members I've interviewed, honesty, integrity, compassion, willingness to work hard, willingness to take a good risk now and then, a generous heart, and devotion to family are universally praised as essential to a vital life. This was illustrated particularly well by Charlie's story.

Charlie was born in Hawaii where his dad served as a Korean attaché. When he was nine months old, they returned to Korea for a few years. The rest of his life was spent mostly in the US. His given name was Korean, but since he lived in the US, his name was Americanized and he became Charlie. His wife asked him once if he would be Charles in business and he said no, he was Charlie. He was down-to-earth and liked people to be comfortable around him.

In the prime of life, Charlie had a loving wife and young children, a successful and promising career working with people who respected him, his parents and siblings were alive and well, he had many friends, he traveled extensively with his family, and they had wonderful adventures across the globe. Charlie and his family enjoyed each other. Life was going well.

Most families I work with are bringing an elderly member of the family to rest, but ultimately death does not discriminate. Even though we all know we will cross over at some point, it still comes as a shock when someone we know gets a much shorter timeline than we anticipate. For Charlie, death struck him down in what many would describe as the peak of life. When he died at the age of fifty-two after fighting an illness, his family and friends were in deep grief.

When I stepped into Charlie's home, I began as I always do with expressing condolences for their loss. I gathered the names of everyone present and their connections to Charlie. I gave them a moment to slip gently into conversation, so they could take some deep breaths, cry, speak or be silent, shake their heads in disbelief, hug each other, or whatever else they needed.

When they were ready, I began to ask questions. What I heard about was a happy life. Debbie said that Charlie kept them on track. He made a point of keeping his family close, including sitting down for dinner together, joking together, and sharing adventures.

One of their favorite places was the mountains. Charlie loved to take his family skiing and on hikes. He would let his family ski down a hill first, and then came Charlie, dashing down the slope at lightning pace, sometimes even whipping through trees. When they were hiking, Charlie knew how to read the landscape. (In the high country where the trails are faint or obscured by snow, you must study the terrain for indications on where to go. Sometimes you are guided by cairns.) When they got lost hiking once, he got them over a ridge and back on the trail.

Reading *life's* landscape is an essential skill, too. Charlie showed his children how to do that as well. For example, he and Debbie taught their children how to treat people with courtesy and lift the spirits of those around them.

It's important to have the right supplies for an adventure. A family as energetic as Charlie's, with young kids, needs food on hand to fuel their day. He was the one in charge of the family backpack. Charlie and Debbie carefully packed such wonderful meals that other people coming down the trail or ski slope often stopped to ask what they were having for lunch because it smelled bold and wonderful. A home-cooked lunch with yummy Korean flavors is a lot better than an energy bar.

In every conceivable way, Charlie was deliciously prepared to share each day with his family.

Their memories of what it was like to be with Charlie told me that he knew more than how to go down a mountain. Charlie showed his family how to live. Debbie said that he was the one to "reel them in" by making sure they had spent time together and laughed together. It's common for grieving hearts to gravitate toward good memories, and this family shared many funny moments, silly things that were said, times they sparkled while enjoying their family.

Charlie's backpack was at his funeral, decorated with flowers and encircled by candles. His children lit the candles, one by one, while we considered the skills and resources Charlie left as his legacy to them. A family member called his children "light bearers."

My tribute to Charlie compared his family's memories to a "spiritual backpack" that was filled with essential life lessons that will guide his children for years to come: generosity, strength, humor, creativity, fun, resourcefulness, a commitment to enjoying life, fairness and honesty, determination, resilience, and love of family.

I included the backpack in the ceremony because I hoped that it would be a helpful metaphor as his wife and children returned to lives without Charlie physically present. They would miss Charlie deeply, but they would not be adrift, because he had pointed them in a good direction and provided the character resources and love to continue, supporting each other along the way.

When we walk in a purposeful direction, our path can both sustain us and indicate how we will be remembered. Nothing about this pertains to financial comfort. It is within the capability of each of us to intentionally form a positive legacy of character whether or not we are wealthy. Charlie had a clear image of what was needed to sustain his family.

If he could have been at his own memorial service, Charlie's message would have sounded something like this: "Keep walking. Your path might not always be clear, but you have the means to find your path and the energy to walk it. Enjoy life! I left guiding lights for you: lights of character, love for each other, and laughter. Keep going toward them."

The Continental Divide includes some long roads extending to the horizon.

Nana, ninety-seven years

Another story from a good life brought me to reflect on the effect of enduring love in a family.

"Nana" (the name her grandchildren gave her) grew up on a Nebraska farm in the years of the Great Depression. She mentioned having pigeon soup in those lean years. Surely her childhood taught Nana how to weather the bumps in life's road;

when something unexpected and troublesome happened, she calmed the family down with some of her favorite expressions: "Horsefeathers!" and "That's life!"

Nana's passing did not leave anyone in shock, because she had lived a full life—close to a century. Her family was greatly saddened, of course. The figure who had been at the center of their family life for five generations was gone.

When Nana married George in the 1950s, he was a widower with a child who required special care. Nana devoted herself to this child's care for many years, long after all their other children were grown and George had passed away. When George died, she lost the love of her life with whom she had shared more than forty years of a happy marriage. Nana would sometimes sit quietly and play his favorite songs on an old record player, missing George deeply. Her family worried about her, but perhaps they needn't have, because Nana wasn't one to lose track of her purpose in life—taking care of her family.

Time and again, Nana gave the gift of her presence and rallied the family's spirits. When her great-granddaughter was born prematurely, with complications, Nana set herself up at the neonatal unit to hold this tiny baby, rock her, and tell her repeatedly how much she was loved. Before the end of Nana's days, she had a great-great-grandchild, too. All the generations were represented at the ceremony honoring Nana's life.

Dear Nana made certain the members of her family never lost sight of the importance of their family being rooted in love. On Nana's watch, family squabbles were put to rest, and everyone made time to gather. It was common knowledge that everybody was expected to show up at Nana's house on Christmas Eve. And unless a baby was being born that day, they all did show up. At the holidays and at every special occasion or spontaneous get-together, Nana cooked for everybody. A handwritten note on a board in her kitchen said, "LOVE—you don't leave Nana's house without it."

By the time Nana passed away, she had instilled in her family the value of persevering love. It had held her family together for almost a hundred years. When I last saw them, they were heading home for a big family dinner and sharing memories spanning the five generations that Nana presided over.

Nana's story showed me the sustaining power of love that perseveres across generations and extends to the horizon of time.

Chang, eighty-seven years

Some of the most inspiring stories of vision, grace and hope came from families I've worked with who immigrated to this country. Dr. Chang (called Chang by his friends) had grown up in Taiwan when it was occupied by the Japanese in World War II. His childhood memories included sitting with his brother on the hillside outside their home watching American bombs drop on the town below.

Growing up, Chang was diligent in his studies and in growing his Christian faith—both important components of his family's life. How could he have known where this would take him and his family? In 1950, along came a chance connection to "angels"—he caught the attention of a missionary family who sponsored his admission to Goshen, a Christian college in Indiana. Inspired by Chang, one of his brothers also embarked on college in the US five years later. With these young men came a family's hopes and dreams.

Chang's family acknowledged his focus and strict determination.

Knowing him to be a man of faith, they also saw spiritual grace in Chang's remarkable life. After he came to America, he completed his undergraduate studies. He was planning to attend a master's program at the University of Michigan but was diagnosed with tuberculosis.

He had no money to travel nor pay for his care, so the congregation at Goshen collected money from its members to pay for his travel to Denver for treatment. In Denver, additional help came from National Jewish Hospital, whose benefactors paid for 100 percent of his care and made sure he was fed well for several months so he could safely undergo surgery. His care during recovery, which took almost three years, was also provided under the umbrella of the hospital—at no cost. The congregation at Goshen continued to send him money every month so he could buy candies, books, and other things to help him continue to adapt to American life while knowing he was loved and supported.

Chang recovered, married, and raised a family in the US. His children readily spoke of his sacrificial devotion to his family and his kindness to all.

Most remarkably from such beginnings, Chang went on to lead the effort to create Aurora Community College. He served as the college's first president and connected his local community with a global community through the Sister Cities Program, all the while looking beyond himself—up to God and out to people.

Chang's vision was for people to learn, fulfill their potential, and experience the interconnectedness of community across the world. Whether he was teaching them to cook Taiwanese dishes, fix a broken piece of equipment, invest wisely, or learn statistics, Chang wanted people to succeed. Those he taught saw in Chang a lifelong drive to learn.

Throughout a life guided by faith, he was aware of the many good-hearted people accompanying him in fulfilling his vision. He literally hummed through his days.

To honor him, one of his sons chose "O Holy Night" to be played during the funeral; Chang liked Christmas hymns and he liked to hum this one in particular all year. The lyrics are full of angels announcing we're never alone, God is near.

Hanging in the ceremony space was this gift from a sister-village in China, commissioned to honor Dr. Chang when a delegation visited Denver during the Chinese Year of the Tiger. On the scroll, this impressive animal strides forward while looking back over one shoulder. In Chinese culture, the tiger is full of life and represents the drive to achieve. It is a symbol of great prowess, fearsome spirit, and determination.

At the close of the ceremony, I connected this animal symbol to Chang with these words: "The tiger is a fighter—clever and

strong, a leader, and often the one out front. Looking back over his shoulder like the tiger in the scroll, a tiger leader says 'Come this way! Let's go!'" Dr. Chang set an example for a path forward. Countless people gladly followed him.

This spectacular tiger scroll, prominent at Dr. Chang's ceremony, was a symbol of his heritage, legacy, and personality.

Chang's children observe a rich blend of cultural traditions connecting them to timeless qualities. His ceremony was held on Chinese New Year, so there was a big Taiwanese feast afterward; I was honored to attend.

For me, Chang represents a person who holds onto a positive vision for the future. Gratitude for sacred grace in the many ways that grace appears. Abiding hope through all circumstances. These were as sustaining to Dr. Chang's life path as water is to the body.

The inspiration from Dr. Chang's life is deeply connected to his consistently walking in the direction of what sustained and inspired him. Indeed, his vision for what was possible set his steps in motion and carried him through all the challenges with grace and hope. No wonder his family and his professional community carry his legacy forward for others to follow.

Laurie, the family member of a person we brought to rest

Not all family histories are uplifting, let alone as inspiring as Dr. Chang's. Many family histories include tragedy and hardship, or experiences that are hurtful, violent, or abusive.

A beautiful woman, Laurie (whose name I have changed) greeted me at the door of her home when I visited her to plan a funeral for her uncle. She had long black hair that fell to her shoulders, a streak of gray in the one lock that crossed her dark eyes, smooth skin that belied her age. She moved with composed grace to the living room, invited me to sit down, then she took a seat across from me. Physically, she looked younger than her years, but she had a spirit that was ages older. She had a look of quiet confidence and the peace that some people who have come to terms with pain and loss exude.

Laurie informed me early in our conversation that her uncle abused children in the family, including her. When I first heard this, I was stunned that she was planning a ceremony for him. For Laurie, the ceremony meant bringing closure to past events, putting the weight down, literally burying them with this individual so she could move on.

None of the abusive experiences were mentioned in the ceremony, but this funeral was her way of saying to her own spirit that the hurtful past was behind her. She was choosing to walk toward a positive family culture. Her face showed this; her intentions were crystal clear. She would banish the darkness in the family's past and bring in an era of light. Indeed, she would find a way to *be* that light.

I'm not a therapist, but my observations lead me to believe it's possible for trauma to subside, one day at a time, with the support of friends and the assistance of professional counselors as needed. Prayer and other means of supporting the spiritual self can bring sacred presence alongside personal resolve. With spiritual support and the practical efforts of people coming alongside those who have been traumatized, grace and hope can find their way into even the darkest corners and lift the people there. May such kindness always be among us.

ON THE TRAIL:
GOOD ROOTS

For one thousand miles of the trail (a third of the entire hike), I was accompanied by my eldest brother, Mike. The two of us and our other brother, Brian, hiked together when we were growing up in California. We shared hair-raising moments and moments of awesome beauty in nature. Those hikes with my brothers were the roots of my love for the outdoors.

They were good roots indeed. In January 2021, I asked Mike, "Would you be interested and available to hike about six hundred miles with me this summer?" Mike was an athlete and consummate outdoorsman all his life; he also loved me, his little sister. There was only a brief moment of silence before Mike replied, "Yeah, I could do that." He later told me it never occurred to him not to join me.

I'm grateful to have grown up in a loving family and to have a sibling who was willing, even in our senior years, to support me in this way. At the time of my call, I was sixty-five and Mike was seventy-five.

Mike and I ran into few sibling hiking teams and none of those teams were close to our ages. We crossed paths with one young man who said his sister was "a hundred miles back!" He said she was okay, but really?

Mike and I hiked together over the course of four summers, facing all the challenges come what may and never barking at each other unless somebody (who was that?) forgot to put their glasses on while reading a map and giving directions. We thought we had an exceptional record for that much time together.

Reconnecting with a sibling for a once-in-a-lifetime experience like this was a gift beyond measure. I'm confident that Nana, who taught her kids and grandkids the value of good family roots and love that goes the distance, would have approved.

When grace shows up

From what I could tell, most hikers on long-distance trails get a trail name if they're hiking the entire trail. I was no exception. Consistent with tradition, I received the name from someone else rather than naming myself. My trail name was Grace. I snagged it immediately when my best friend recommended it, because I didn't want a trail name indicative of something I had done that was embarrassing. Most of all, I liked the aspirational implications of "grace." There are many definitions—all of them positive. I knew that name would inspire me to be a better person on the trail. I wanted to be glad about how grace or Grace showed up.

A perspective on grace applied to my hopes and expectations each day I was hiking. By myself or with partners, I moved forward every day with a goal in mind. But having clear intentions to reach a goal doesn't mean we're in control of everything that happens. When what happened on the trail was outside my control and problematic, I needed some grace to show up.

A hiking partner and I were in dire need of water north of Pie Town, New Mexico, when we came to a source that we were counting on; it was dry. There were only a few cars passing by each hour, but within minutes the couple who owned the ranch nearby pulled up beside us in their pickup truck. They clarified directions to the next water source and gave us a bottle of water for the walk. Their hospitality was perfectly timed; we were in the presence of grace. Like what Chang experienced, angels in human form showed up to help. They renewed our hope and our resolve. The water down the road was plentiful.

I took this as a lesson on mindset: Remain determined to move forward but also be open to grace. It's amazing how that mindset renews strength to continue and builds anticipation that all will be well.

The following day, we had enough water to stay hydrated, but when a US Forest Service truck stopped and the crew asked if we needed water, I accepted a bottle and dumped it on my head. Never turn down water in a desert! This was my little celebration of a gracious gift on a hot day.

Pie Town, New Mexico, is a tiny community with a lot of delicious pie, which is a hit with hungry hikers.

The days of searching for water on the trail, and experiences of being blessed by family and by generous strangers, opened my heart to appreciate what life stories were also telling me: Set out with intention to search for what is vital, bring all of my best self to the effort, anticipate and even invite help in difficult times, hold onto my vision and, like a ray of light, be a hopeful person, persevere in love for this wild experience called life, and be grateful (celebrate!) when grace appears.

FOR READER REFLECTION

- *Who are the elders in your family (perhaps that includes you), and what are the elders teaching next generations about character?*

- *Do your family roots include experience of love that endures across generations? Has that guided you in any way?*

- *If considering your roots is painful for you, what new perspectives are you developing for a better history moving forward?*

- *What is your experience of grace: generosity of heart, unexpected moments of being cared for, or perhaps awareness of being accompanied by a presence beyond yourself and your loved ones?*

- *How do you hope your family will describe you when they look back at your life one day? Are you intentionally walking toward the person you would like to become?*

For reasons we might never know, some carry more in this life than others do. Stories at the next waypoint consider how we carry hurts, loss, challenges, and disappointments.

TRAVEL LIGHTLY

Backpackers are rightly obsessed with the weight of their pack. The rule of thumb is to try not to carry more than a quarter of your body weight. Following the experience of carrying about forty pounds in the New Mexico desert, I was bent and in pain. Weighing in around 116 at the start and inevitably dropping weight on the trail, I had far too much on my back. I learned from suffering and quickly shed what I didn't need. With rare exception on long hauls, my full pack with food and water for five days shrunk to under thirty pounds.

My brother Mike learned his lesson on pack weight the second summer we hiked together. This was to be our longest trek, and Mike learned the difference between how a pack feels when you try it on in your kitchen versus when it's on your back for more than five hundred miles. Our first break was at Camp Sula, Montana. I can see it now: He leaned on the bunk bed and said that he didn't know it would be like this. He was referring to carrying a burdensome pack a considerable distance in arduous conditions. (Some of the conditions were downright unpleasant.)

To his credit, Mike sat down on the deck of the cabin and started pulling things out of his pack. A heavy knife our dad gave him and even peanut M&Ms went into a discard pile. (My daughter quipped, "Uncle Mike had more stuff in that bag than Mary Poppins." It's been a family joke ever since.) The extra "stuff" either went in a hiker box for other hikers to pick through at the campground or it was boxed up and mailed home. For the next eight hundred miles, Mike's pack was as light as it could be.

Now we had a guiding metaphor set in our bodies: Get rid of what you don't need to carry.

In the lives of those I was called upon to memorialize, the people who adapted well to life knew how to set aside things that might pull them back.

Bonnie's story stood out as an example of someone who chose to dance through her days. She lived in the presence of a vivid symbol of her own bright response to life's uncertainties.

Bonnie, ninety years

Bonnie, another child of the Great Depression in Nebraska, grew up to enjoy the finer things in life.

Because of Bonnie, there was more color and beauty in the world. She was elegant in her personal appearance, home, and garden. With striking white hair in her senior years, Bonnie was well-dressed, composed, and witty; she was a beautiful presence. She was also dignified on a deeper level: a gracious person who understood that relationships are important. She enjoyed being with people. The youngest members of the family thought of her as a "cool grandma" who liked making them laugh.

Beneath Bonnie's beautiful life, however, was considerable loss.

Bonnie had experienced the death of children, her husband, and her siblings in the prime years of her life. Notably, she chose to go through her life graciously. She held no grudges. She was happy. She laughed readily. She had a special interest in the arts and gave art history lessons to her grandchildren; I think she indirectly tutored them in the art of joy.

For many years, Bonnie had a Tiffany window in her home. By all accounts, it was a masterpiece of artistic expression in stained glass. It now hangs in the Boston Museum of Fine Arts where the public enjoys it every day—*Parakeets and Gold Fish Bowl*. But when it hung in her home, this glorious work of art was in a special room for Bonnie and her family's enjoyment. She liked to sit with her window, never tiring of its beauty. She often invited her grandchildren into that space to talk about it. Even with the pain of loss inside her, she retained her dignified, caring character and was at peace. She chose to love life rather than live in pain.

The window depicts parakeets clowning around in a tree. The playful scene also has an edge to it: Hanging amid the birds is a fishbowl. Some of the birds are staring at it. One can assume that the fish were not impressed with the birds at play, but rather afraid of being violently plucked from the bowl. As one who appreciated art, Bonnie appreciated beauty, but she also knew the dangerous aspects of life. She experienced firsthand the proximity of death and the violent intrusion death can be in an imagined life. Even so, the impression of Bonnie—as with this window—was exuberant and full of life.

At the memorial service honoring her, I left the family with an image of Bonnie in her new home: on the other side of this life, greeted by those who arrived before her, looking back at us as if through a colorful crystal window. What hadn't been clear during her times of suffering has been resolved, even made joyful. Would the picture have been less vibrant without the stirred-up waters of the fishbowl? Yes. But what would life be without awareness of the possibility of loss?

To experience life's dangers and loss and yet choose to see joy through your personal window, is a deeply transformative choice.

We choose what we carry, even when we don't fully understand why we've gone through what we did. With time and our choices, love for life transforms us.

Clayton, sixty-nine years

Someone who can laugh at a lot of life is someone with a big heart.

His family called Clayton "a jolly man, a big teddy bear with a little growl." He loved his family and worked hard for them throughout his life. His practice was to consider carefully what he wanted, then save for it and get it. Although thrifty, he was capable of buying something extravagant like a big comfortable vehicle for everybody in the family to take a trip in.

He also enjoyed a good story. Like men in the television westerns he liked to watch, he was a salt-of-the-earth, happy man.

Countless times when I have interviewed families in preparation for a funeral, the conversation turns to lighthearted moments. A grieving heart often gravitates to happy moments, especially times of laughing together. The family loved sharing the following story with me.

Clayton drove a bus for the city of Denver. One night on the way back to the garage when the bus was empty, Clayton got hungry. As he was driving by a McDonald's, he decided he wanted a burger. McDonald's drive-throughs are not built to handle **a bus**, so Clayton and the bus got stuck. The fellows back at the garage never let him live that down. Imagine the phone conversation when he called headquarters to say he needed help. "You're not going to believe this, but I'm stuck in line at McDonald's."

Clayton was also remembered for deciding what he *didn't* want. He was a professional wrestler until a moment when he was suspended in mid-air and said to himself, "I could get hurt doing this." He ended his pro-wrestling career on the spot.

This same man who could get himself in comical situations also had a profound depth of character. Clayton was a Black man. He purposely walked into an edgier life when, for love of a good woman, he married Judy, a woman of a different race. She was also a woman of good character—strong and kind. They were absolutely devoted to each other and raised a beautiful family together.

After Judy passed away, he missed her deeply. Just six months after her death, within a few hours of signing some papers to put his affairs in order, Clayton was found completely still in his chair with a big smile on his face. There never was an explanation for the cause of his death; his heart had simply stopped. Judy was known to say, "I've got this," so the family thought Judy had stepped in when she saw he was ready and said these words one more time to him. Off he went, freed from the world like one of the butterflies Judy loved, as light as could be, back to her side.

Not once in my visits with Clayton and Judy's family did they mention the challenges this couple must have faced in an interracial marriage in 1967. What I heard was how they went through life with love and purpose, devotion, courage, and laughter. They were models for all that and more: a light-hearted and caring life underscored by their readiness to laugh.

A mountain meadow in the bloom of summer on the way to Steamboat Springs.

Family memories of Clayton and Judy included ready laughter, but some families' grief is complicated by anger, years of unresolved arguments and estrangement, or perhaps by habits or addictions that deeply hurt people. A family might want the memorial service to acknowledge this so that the ceremony is both authentic to family history and helpful to them in moving forward. Without that, the burden of grief may be painfully extended. It can be cathartic to make space in a funeral service to directly acknowledge the grief and the hole now left in the lives of loved ones. Here we get into the heart of moving beyond complicated grief.

● Carla, seventy-three years

Most of us need some mercy. Finding our way awkwardly through life, carrying our flaws with us, we each need some measure of forgiveness.

But how do loved ones resolve estrangements and sad feelings after someone is gone? Like a backpacker carrying unnecessary weighty stuff, we need to consider what we're carrying emotionally and manage to somehow shed what we are burdened with.

When I'm aware that a death has left behind conflicted feelings in a family, with frustration and hurt mixed in with their grief, I ask the family if I may include a forgiveness ritual in the memorial service. The words I use are a variation on a mantra that originated with the Ho'oponopono,* a native culture of Hawaii, for healing relationships through forgiveness. The family of a colleague of mine added universally familiar words to create a new mantra for healing complicated grief; I added a simple ritual to accompany those words. My hope is to bring some peace to the grieving family by acknowledging their hurt

---

* The list of statements in the forgiveness ritual of the Ho'oponopono Healing Ceremony are "I love you, I'm sorry, Please forgive me, and Thank you." These words intended for healing relationships through seeking and receiving forgiveness have been brought to public attention by several spiritual and self-help leaders. A funeral setting where relationships need healing is different; someone has departed, and a mantra's words should consider the possibility that those who are feeling hurt did not do anything wrong. The combination of basic words into a mantra is powerful. The words were adapted for funerals where the words could be helpful—"Thank you, I'm sorry, I forgive you, I accept, I love you."

and giving them a visual symbol for putting down the burden on their heart. The following is an example.

Carla and her twin sister were born in Denver. She lived there almost all her life. In her youth, she loved to take care of children. She pursued this interest into adulthood by caring for children of all ages and was particularly gifted with infants. Carla gave more than a hundred kids a good start in life.

Her legacy also included a quick wit; Carla could always find something funny to say about any situation, even difficult ones. Her son Andrew recalled a lot of laughter in the family when he was growing up.

Her legacy also included her love of music, which influenced Drew tremendously, including his choice of a career.

Sadly, medical conditions caused Carla to be in pain and fatigued all her adult life. As she aged, Carla avoided closeness with people and isolated herself. She used to say, "Love many, trust few, always paddle your own canoe." But paddling your canoe alone can be lonely and difficult. She became increasingly private and wary. People continued to extend their love to Carla, but sometimes got their feelings hurt because she had isolated herself.

After deliberating on how to address the complexities in his mother's life, Drew included these words in our ceremony for her: "Carla was not oblivious to the kindness that was given to her. But, not wanting to be vulnerable, she kept people at arm's distance, for reasons her surviving loved ones may never completely understand."

Carla was a marvel as a gardener. In a ritual that acknowledged her wondrous skill with plants, I spoke the words below to those who gathered to honor her life.

> When we're faced with the loss of someone we love, it's not uncommon for there to be a mixture of feelings, some of them in conflict with each other. I offer this: Love is far stronger than any response it might receive, including a hurtful response or silent isolation. Love is, after all, far stronger even than death.
>
> Each of us needs a measure of *love and mercy* from those we leave behind. Carla now needs, and in the end we all do, a garden of kindness and mercy like the beautiful gardens she grew. [I put a small pot with soil on a silver tray next to the podium and planted a tiny garden of crocuses—one bulb for each of the following.]
>
> I pray that there will be a time—if not today, then when you're ready—for family and friends to say this to Carla in your hearts:
>
> - **Thank you** *for your lively, interesting friendship, for welcoming friends into conversation, and for a wit that brought laughter to so many people. Thank you also for your incredible legacy of loving so many children at the start of their lives. And thank you for loving your own children.*
> - **I'm sorry** *that you so often felt anxious and afraid of being too close to someone.*
> - **I forgive you** *for the times of confusion and hurt.*

- **I accept** *that there were things I didn't understand and can't change. And for my own sake, I either smile at those or I put them down.*
- **I love you.**

Life is messy. [I brushed the dirt from my fingers.] When any of us departs this world, we leave behind interactions that need one of these responses from the people that we were close to: "Thank you, I'm sorry, I forgive you, I accept what I can't change, and I love you."

The tenderness you find in letting go of burdens and turning to each other will see you through all things. You were there for Carla. Trust that she knew you cared. [I then put out a pot of

blooming crocuses next to the pot with planted bulbs, as a symbol of the beauty that is possible with time.]

May you find peace in knowing that Carla is at peace, without anxiousness, pain, or earthly turmoil.

A crocus is often the first flower to poke out of the snowy Colorado mud in spring.

Over time, happy memories of her will bloom in your hearts.

I've used this ritual for other families, adapting the words of the mantra to fit each family's situation.

> We don't always know why things happen the way they do or why people make the choices they make. But we can find relief from our questions and hurt by putting our broken feelings in the holy dirt of forgiveness and believing it will bloom in a lightened heart.

Jim, twenty-five years

Jim's story gave me insight into the importance of sharing each other's burdens, which a lightened life requires.

Jim was born in Englewood, a suburb of Denver, and was an energetic and intelligent child. He joined a swim team when he was five. When he was in first grade and the teacher asked him to come over to her, he did barrel rolls to cross the room. When his mom couldn't find him in the yard, it was likely that Jim was up a tree. When Jim was taking ski lessons during a family ski outing, he chose to lay on the mountain in his own world, vigorously making snow angels.

Even as a youngster, Jim was acutely aware that his experience of life was different.

Learning how to relate to personal energy and the energy in the universe was an important part of Jim's life. He was attuned to the energy around him—it was his gift. Jim excelled at intuiting what someone else needed and sending his energy to help them—often resulting in perfect results for the other person and in benefits to Jim as well. But there was a shadow side to this gift; Jim worried about sustaining his skills of perception and was afraid of letting people down.

Diagnosed with bipolar disorder, Jim's experience of life was torn by fear and frustration. He expressed how difficult his life was because friends didn't understand what he was experiencing because he "looked" normal. His family tried many ways to help him over the years. But he felt he couldn't continue in such pain. He knew he would be hurting people he loved by leaving them, but he felt he was also hurting them by the way he was living. At the age of twenty-five, Jim took his life.

Despite the brevity of Jim's time among us, his legacy was rich, full of beloved memories of his funny and whimsical side (he could speak in a made-up language, for example), his acute understanding of others, and his kindness.

Following a suicide by a young person, not only is everyone at the memorial service in deep mourning, many are also thinking about the young people in the room, hoping they will not repeat this choice. While preparing the service for Jim, I was intent on taking care of his family, but I also thought a lot about Jim's friends who would be there.

The day before the funeral I continued my preparations by going out for a long and difficult hike up a mountain: more than three thousand feet of elevation gain, summiting above twelve thousand feet, and hiking seventeen miles roundtrip. With those teens and younger adults in mind, I purposely made my trek steeper, higher, and longer than usual.

While I was deep in thought on the trail, two words came to me: Choose life. Almost immediately, I rounded a corner and came upon a sparkling, beautiful field of rose quartz. Rose quartz is thought to be energetically connected to the heart, which I thought would be meaningful to Jim. Without thinking more than a second about it, I put six of the pink stones in my pack. I should *not* have taken anything from the trail—and I would normally not do this—but in a moment full of emotion, I took the stones. They were each about the size of my palm, large enough for me to feel their weight. Some of them had lichen on them, clinging to life.

His parents approved my acknowledging during the ceremony that their son had ended his life, and they knew I would address his friends. At the end of the ceremony celebrating all the beautiful aspects of Jim's life, I turned my attention to the youngest people in the room. I told the story of the rose quartz. I put the stones on the table and said:

> A person that just met you *this week* was willing to load her pack with stones and carry a burden up a mountain for you. How much more willing would the person sitting next to you be to carry a burden for you? That person might have known you your entire life. How willing would they be to carry your burdens? Of course they would be willing to do that for you. Of course they would.
>
> When you are low, in need of strength, in need of "a rock" for support, or even a cairn of rocks to guide you down the trail that you've lost sight of, remember to "choose life," and live it to the fullest extent that you can.
>
> Those who love you will be your rock or help you find the cairns to guide your way. The energy of life is in the person next to you and all around you in this universe, and that energy is a *loving* energy, bursting out in even very tough situations. That love is ready to give you what you need to hang on and to choose life.

Jim's friends and parents took the stones home. When I was alone, I broke down. I prayed these kids would remember to turn to a family member or friend and not carry their burdens alone.

ON THE TRAIL:
PUT DOWN WHAT DOESN'T SERVE YOU

Every experienced backpacker knows how to go through their pack and get rid of stuff they don't need and don't want to carry. And every backpacker spends a lot of time in their thoughts. The trail helped me to get better at recognizing weighty stuff I was carrying in my thoughts. It's not good to carry grudges. It's much better to forgive and forget.

I spent a summer hiking with someone who couldn't stop picking on my gear choices and expressing that pace was critical to her. She was the perfect hiking partner in experience and skill, but I was slower than she was, and I felt like the weak link in our hiking team. Unfortunately and unwisely, I let her critiques burrow into my thoughts and discourage me. My spirit sank. My boots felt like lead weights because I hardly felt like walking. We needed to make an important decision when we came to the pass below Devil's Thumb, on the ridgeline above Nederland, Colorado.

Looking south from that pass, the CDT extends along the ridge to Rogers Pass, ascends over James Peak, stays high above the trees to Berthoud Pass, dips briefly, then returns to the alpine for several miles beyond that.

Exposure on high points above trees (the alpine zone) presents a particularly high risk when lightning is in the area; when we got near Devil's Thumb, a storm was coming in. I didn't think we could find a place to safely come down off the trail before the storm would be on us. But I was also acutely aware that escape meant not completing that portion of the CDT, which was difficult to reach.

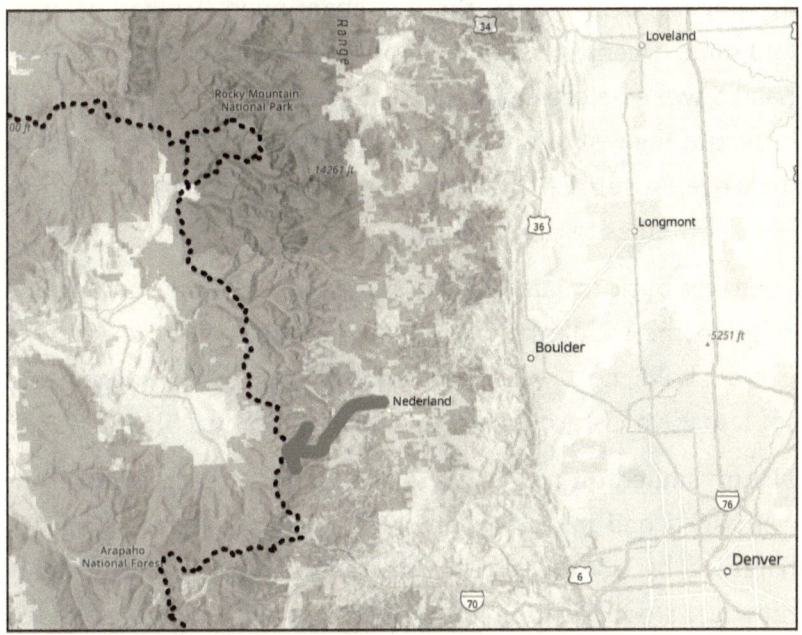

The arrow points to the approximate location of the ridgeline in this story.

When we sat down to discuss what to do, she said, "I'm sorry you'll have to give up on your dream." I wasn't sure what she meant. Seeing my puzzled look, she said, "I'm sorry you have to give up hiking the CDT." I was shocked. I felt that her choice of words meant more than postponing this portion for our safety. What I heard, instead, was that she thought I might have to give up my dream of completing the CDT because I didn't have what it took to finish the trail. Silently, I committed to proving her wrong.

We took a different route down from the ridge and into the trees to avoid the storm. While we hiked, I was thinking about how I could return and complete that ridgeline myself.

A few weeks later, when sunny skies were forecast for the day, I drove into the mountains west of Rollinsville, Colorado, near the portion of the CDT that we abandoned. I hiked a quick four-mile ascent in the afternoon and set up camp at Rogers Lake. I woke before dawn the next day. With a day pack on my back and the rest of my gear hanging from a tree, I sprinted to the ridge. At sunrise, I was standing at Rogers Pass with James Peak two miles to the south.

I put my back to James Peak and sped eight miles along the ridge to the saddle below Devil's Thumb—where my hiking partner told me I wouldn't complete the CDT. I tagged that spot, made a U-turn, and returned to my camp.

Nature smiled on me: I was gifted an image of freedom from criticism I had taken too much to heart. A peregrine falcon, harassed by a crow, put the crow in his place with a lightning-fast stoop, dropping out of the sky with its wings folded back in a straight-line plummet toward what was pestering him. It was breathtaking to watch. I came out of my dark thoughts and called all my abilities to the forefront.

I made it back to my home base—a roundtrip of seventeen miles. After lowering my gear from the tree, I put all of it on my back and hustled an additional four miles down the trail to my car, two thousand feet below.

That total twenty-five-mile effort was a turning point. When I filled the hole in that portion of the CDT, my determination was renewed: I was going to complete the entire trail no matter what.

Physical success wasn't the only reason my spirit lightened. The additional reason was forgiveness. I forgave the person who had doubted me, and I released my misgivings about myself. I shouldn't have let someone else's opinion bother me as much as it did. She called it like she saw it, but she was wrong. I needed to live into what I could do. I needed to stop whining and doubting and walk into what was in front of me. That's all. Move on.

The following summer, negative perspectives banished, I embarked on my longest solo hike: north from Grand Lake, Colorado, across the Wyoming border to Battle Pass—a total of 177 miles. I dodged storms and moose, crossed over the shoulder of Mount Zirkle, traversed peaks and remote terrain with no one in sight, all the while telling myself, "You know how to do this. Now go do it!"

Above my camp at Rogers Lake, heading up to the CDT on the ridgeline.

My self-image had opened to possibilities; I was lighter and ready to move.

Almost in Wyoming.

Sharing from abundance

The trail also taught me that sometimes we need to share what might help somebody else. On the trail, you shouldn't ask people to carry your pack, let alone your body, unless you're badly wounded. I once witnessed a group of young bucks, proud to say they were accountants, carry a young woman down the trail from the summit of a peak. She had an ankle injury and couldn't walk, and these half-dozen hearty dudes contributed their strength to get her down the mountain. I was so impressed by their high-spirited generosity that I called their boss the next day to tell him about their effort.

More frequent, though, were opportunities to share light things I was carrying for hundreds of miles and someone else needed: that piece of duct tape I wrapped around my trekking pole that could repair their tent, that spare buckle that could fix a pack strap, the extra carabiner that someone could use to hang their food up a tree so a bear wouldn't get it, the supply of magnesium pills that help me sleep—it could be anything! Someone else is in need. Give it away.

Maybe in the grand scheme of things that's why that spare item was with me to begin with—because somebody else would need it. Every time I shared in this way or witnessed someone else share something at the end of long, tiresome hours carrying a pack on the trail, there were smiles and laughter. Hikers' spirits were lighter.

On the trail, I also thought about Jim. He carried the heavy burden of having bipolar disorder, but he also carried his gifts for perceiving what was troubling people and levity. He shared both in abundance. How amazingly beautiful that this person who felt the pain of being in dark places, frightened and frustrated, gave himself to help other people or share a whimsical moment. In the light of such inspiration, we can *all* be more generous.

Angels

A trail angel is someone who aids hikers on long-distance trails. Trail angels for me and my hiking partners included three family members and a few friends, but the rest were strangers. All along the way, generous people provided transportation, let us shower at their house, let us sleep on their lawn or in actual beds, fed us, drove us to trailheads, gave us directions to stores and laundromats, listened to our stories, and lifted our spirits.

In Montana alone, where logistics are especially tricky because of the long distances between towns, *eleven people* helped my brother and me to cross their state.

Small courtesies were treasures. A cup of tea offered by a couple from Georgia was a cup of golden warmth. After hiking seventeen miles, I arrived at the pass where they were parked when a slurry of sleet descended. But I was warm and dry in the back of their truck with a cup of tea in hand.

My best friend, Kimra (far left), and her husband, Randy (far right), drove all the way from the foothills of Denver to West Yellowstone to bring us a resupply box and cheer us on.

What these people did changed the nature of our adventure. Without them, packs would have been heavier, or we would have been exhausted, or we would have been freezing cold, or burning hot, or treks might not have happened at all. I'm grateful to all of them and found ways to let them know.

Gratitude was just as important as other preparations were to my taking in my surroundings. I made it my practice to talk to the holy source of all I was walking through, to ask for safe travels, open myself to new experiences, and name what we needed on any given day—physical strength, insight to alternative routes, care going through storms, ease in finding water, and occasionally unbounded speed. And finishing each day reflecting on what I was grateful for set me up for the next day: reaching my goals safely, having many terrific encounters, and arriving with a light heart.

The welling up of gratitude for experiences on the trail spilled over into honoring lives through the memorial services I wrote. No matter how beautiful or tragic, smooth or cracked and smudged around the edges, there are elements of beauty and graciousness in each person's life story. There is even something to be grateful for in each life. In the most challenging

cases, there is at least something to be grateful for in the goodness that grew around them. Goodness was sometimes close
to the surface and sometimes buried deep, but from a place of
gratitude, amazing things came to light.

Laughter's superpower

While hiking with my daughter and son-in-law in Glacier
National Park, we came to a high pass after a pleasant morning of moderate ascents. As we sat down for lunch, I peered
around the corner to see what lay ahead; I blanched. There
was a stiff headwind funneling through the notch at the pass,
and a sharp three-thousand-foot drop beyond. The trail tra-
versing the face was quite narrow or occasionally washed out,
which required a short leap to keep going. I turned to Zach,
who was getting his lunch out of his pack, and said, "Put that
back, we need to go." Startled, he asked, "Why, what's up?"
My reply left no doubt. "If we stay here, fear is going to get the
best of me. We need to go *now*." He packed up immediately.
The three of us put on an additional layer for warmth, rounded
the boulder we were sitting behind, faced purposefully into the
wind, and took off.

I was in the lead and going at the top speed I could muster.
"Mom!" my daughter shouted from behind. "You're practically
running!" In a moment of insight, I yelled back, "I need to set
the pace so the wind doesn't set it for me!" I braced the gusts,
and Zach grabbed the lid buckle on my backpack in order to
steady me as we jogged down the trail. With all of us leaning
forward and angling one shoulder into the wind, he started
singing. His rallying anthem of choice was the theme song from
the adventure movie *Raiders of the Lost Ark*. I started laughing.

It was a brilliant diversion. You can't be afraid if you're laughing. That melody instantly became the family theme song for adventure. When I hear it now, it still makes me laugh.

I think dear Clayton, whom I honored for his devotion to Judy and for their life of love and laughter, would appreciate how laughter helped me overcome fear. And I appreciate how his story inspires me to this day to laugh and love. From Clayton especially I learned that people are often remembered for the laughter they share—such a gift to those they have loved.

Joy as an art

Mike and I were more than halfway through the Bob Marshall Wilderness in northern Montana when I heard the laughter and shouts of several children. I had *never* heard such a sound deep in the wilderness.

There was a large family— the Netteburgs—on this trail, but I thought they were in New Mexico. A mom and dad plus their five children ranging in age from an infant to thirteen were on the CDT in 2022. As I later learned, they had flipped north from New Mexico to continue hiking while snow melted in Colorado. There they were, trotting by our campsite—all seven of them!

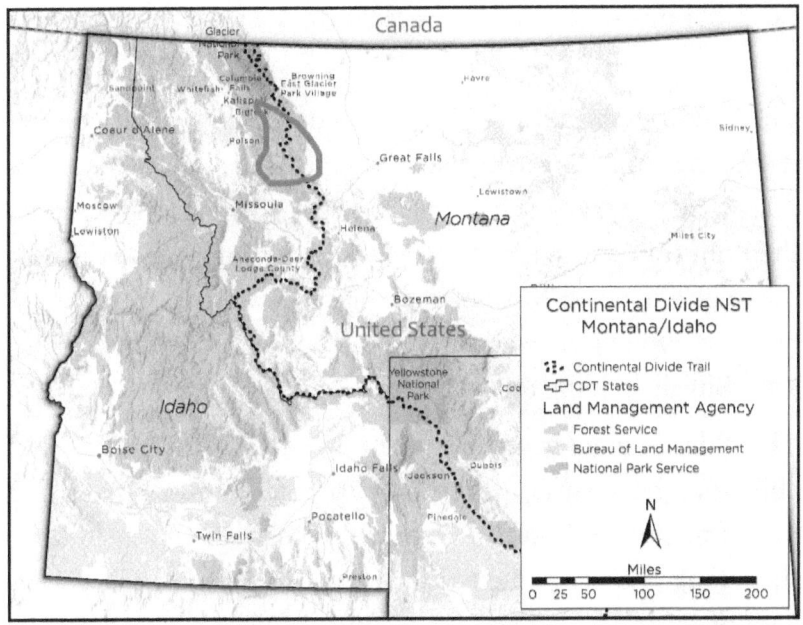

*The circle roughly outlines the Bob Marshall Wilderness in Montana—
northeast of Missoula, southeast of Kalispell and Flathead Lake.*

The Netteburgs with Mike and me.

Their baby was given the trail name "Dead Weight," which says
something about this family's humor.

The Netteburgs became well-known on social media while
they were hiking the Appalachian Trail. A large family with
young children completing long-distance trails is remarkable.

But what made a lasting impression on me was *how* they were doing this.

There was such joy among them—you could hear it coming down the trail. The Facebook group for the CDT hikers of 2022 had several comments from hikers who encountered them on trail and were so impressed by them. For the rest of the hike, whenever Mike or I felt like grumbling as we crawled over a downed tree, we'd turn to each other incredulously and say, "But she's doing this with a baby on her back!"

The oldest daughter set the pace for the day. All the kids had child-size backpacks, not makeshift cutesy things that were meant to carry schoolbooks. And they all had chores. It took them longer to get going in the morning, but then they covered a lot of ground, sometimes continuing until sunset.

Some of the things they were carrying amazed us. Mom carried a small potty seat to potty train her one-year-old. When we caught up with them one afternoon, the baby was on a potty in the middle of the trail. I had never encountered potty-training on the trail! Meanwhile, Dad was carrying a big bag of marshmallows so they could have s'mores that night—highly unusual in the backcountry but custom-made to keep the kids' spirits up after a long day hiking.

What stood out most was their spirit. Each time we ran into the Netteburg family, cheerfulness surrounded them. Every hiker who mentioned them noticed the same thing: They left a positive, energetic, joy-filled impression as they passed by.

The mother and father, Danae and Olen, are both physicians in Chad, one of the poorest countries in the world. They have witnessed many tragedies in their many years as medical missionaries for the Seventh-day Adventist Church. These long hikes each year are family time and important breaks from their stressful life. Between hikes, they go back to work and the kids to their studies. Coming out of difficult and sad situations that exceed what I can imagine, they are some of the most lighthearted people I have ever met.*

Perhaps, like Bonnie lived a full life while sharing her Tiffany window, there is an art to joy: Joy can be created by the very process of seeking it out and sharing it. Who could question what a gift that is?

---

* The Netteburgs became what is known as "Triple Crowners," having completed the three longest trails in the US: the twenty-two-hundred-mile Appalachian Trail in 2020, the thirty-one-hundred-mile CDT in 2022, and the twenty-six-hundred-mile Pacific Crest Trail in 2023. They have inspired a lot of hikers, including this author.

FOR READER REFLECTION

Forgiveness

- *Has someone in your life mislabeled your abilities? How did you overcome that? Did you put down the hurt at some point and forgive them?*

- *How will you remember someone who hurt you during their life and has passed away? How will you come to the point you can carry your remembrances lightly, so that you may heal?*

- *Is there someone living whom you have been estranged from and hope to reconcile with? If this is your hope, how might you begin that conversation?*

Sharing

- *Have you "carried" someone when they couldn't move forward in life without help? Has someone done this for* **you***? How did these moments make you feel?*

- *What effects have you seen when you share lighthearted parts of yourself?*

- *Think about when you have shared something you possess (physically or in experience) that someone else needs. How can you open other opportunities to share in this way?*

Gratitude

- *Are there people who were pivotal in your life that you have not expressed your thanks to? What might that mean to them, and to you, if you circled back and thanked them?*

- *When you think of people in your life who have passed away, what about them are you most grateful for?*

- *What effects does sharing gratitude have—on you and others?*

Joy

- *Some people regularly write down what they are grateful for because this awareness transforms their attitude. What connections do you find between gratitude and joy in your life?*

At the next waypoint we'll consider this: What will be the trail that winds through your life? You can determine that. It will be made of small but meaningful moments.

LIVE INTO THE
LITTLE MOMENTS

Some of the most impactful moments don't look immediately like grand achievements, equivalent to reaching a summit that overlooks huge vistas. Rather, the
most impactful moments are often intimate, one-on-one
interactions.

I recall my surprised reaction to my daughter, Grete, when we
were in a notch between two peaks ascending Uncompahgre
Mountain in southern Colorado. The weather was misera-
ble. A gale was blowing, and we were being pelted by side-
ways-blasting sleet. Grete was ahead of me by a few yards
when she turned around and shouted over the howling wind,
"Isn't this fun?!" She meant it! She felt this moment was thrill-
ing and joyous. But fun was *not* how I would have described
the moment.

We reached the summit above fourteen-thousand feet with Grete verbally pulling me up the last hundred yards.

After going back down the mountain, a debate ensued about what "fun" is. We didn't achieve consensus until we agreed that it was amazing to experience "the mountain being a mountain." Yes—though I didn't feel it a few hours before in the sleet—climbing that mountain *was* great fun. As the photo shows, I even laughed. Good for her for reminding me that it's not uncommon for fun to be tied to something uncomfortable. On a mountain or in a relationship—including a mother-daughter relationship—sometimes you have to hang in there. Have faith; it's the laughter that will stick in memory.

A few years later, it was my daughter's turn to be caught off guard. She was surprised when I hopped off a boardwalk in a Montana marsh to snatch a small frog that was a few steps away. There was a young child nearby and I didn't want to miss the opportunity to show the small creature to her. The frog was compliant, the little girl and her mom were happy to see him up close, the frog swam away in perfect form afterward, and my daughter and I smiled about our interactions with a frog and the strangers we shared the trail with. The day's events were born from curiosity and joy, a good combination. These moments came back to me in a way that I didn't foresee.

Years later, a different frog (I presume) was protecting her eggs in the pool of a Montana stream when I stooped down to get water. I didn't snatch up this one. (Do frogs perpetually smile? Or is that a grimace?)

Back at work on ceremonies, the scene with my daughter near the top of a mountain debating what's fun, and the moment I snatched up a frog, came to mind when I was honoring Roberta, a former teacher.

• Roberta, two weeks shy of eighty years

"Tak for alt." While the literal translation is "Thanks for everything," the meaning is greater. A more accurate translation is "with deep and profound gratitude for the bounty and fullness of life." It is a tradition to carve these words on gravestones in Norway and Denmark not so much as words from the deceased, but as words from their loved ones who wish them rest. Tak for alt on a gravestone expresses a combination of gratitude, farewell, and wish for eternal peace.

On behalf of her Norwegian-heritage family, I spoke these words over Roberta, a woman who loved to explore nature with her elementary school students and with her sons, going into muddy situations to enjoy finding out more about nature.

Roberta's biggest lesson was delivered in *how* she lived, which her family summed up in this way:

> Be a good person. Look on the bright side of everything. "Make it a good day."
>
> Make choices that are good for you. Be good to people. Be a good wife, mother, grandmother, and friend. And specifically, because she had sons, she had some lessons in how men should treat women.
>
> Have fun in life. Roberta was often heard saying *"Isn't this fun?!"* no matter what was going on.
>
> If she knew you, she loved you.

Roberta took changes in life with dignity. Her final lesson to all of us was this: When your time comes, leave this earth with grace and dignity.

Here is an excerpt from the eulogy given by her son Eric.

> If you like me or my brothers, that's because of my mom. When my brothers or I did something we were proud of, that's because of my mom. When we help someone who needs a hand, that's because of my mom. When we have patience and stick to something we don't want to do, that's because of my mom. When we

were growing up and you came to our house, you knew it was a loving home, that was because of my mom.

Me and my brothers were the light of her life. Hugs from her needed no reason and were always given out, always. She was fun and had such a beautiful sense of life. Dishes and vacuuming and laundry could wait.

Such great memories of my mom. There was always time made for us kids. Like going to Wash Park for Huckleberry Finn Days, which she dressed us up for, and one of us always won the contest.

We turned so many pollywogs into frogs over the years. There was always time made to take us crawdad hunting. I don't know how she did it, but she knew where all the frogs and snakes would be. We would catch them and she let us bring them home, turning trash cans into aquariums.

My mom let us be kids. It was no problem to come home dirty; clothes and skin could be cleaned. She could tell we were out doing the most important thing, having fun being kids.

Everyone at her local Safeway loved Roberta; she always had an encouraging word for them. Everyone in the crew Eric supervised loved her; she knew all of them. Every student and every son believed they were Roberta's favorite.

We floated a candle in Roberta's memory in a bowl of water and stones. Like ripples in one of those ponds she loved to explore with her children, ripples continue to extend out from the essence of who Roberta was because of her love "for the bounty and fullness of life." Roberta knew that bounty and fullness are held in the details.

Joe, eighty-seven years

When a family with the last appointment of the day hadn't shown up after more than a half hour, I began to lock up and head home. Then I noticed a car racing through the cemetery. When it stopped in front of the funeral home building where I'd been waiting, two young men jumped out and ran to the door. "Are we too late to see our grandfather?" They had arrived to see someone I will call Joe.

I was glad to reply, "No, not at all. I'll open the room. Joe is still here." We went inside.

The grandsons immediately sat down on the couch next to their grandfather's casket, took out lotto scratch tickets, and began scratching the tickets with coins. I was puzzled but quietly left them alone. When I came back into the room to check on them, I asked how this related to their grandfather, and I invited them to tell me what he was like.

They explained that Granddad had bought lottery tickets for them every weekend. He was a bighearted man who gave his time generously to them, cheered them on, and let them share their worries with him. They appreciated his example of hard work and his example of how to have fun. They were grateful for his humor and willingness to do silly things.

After sharing this with me, they each walked over to their grandfather, bowed their heads in silence for a moment, and put a few tickets in his jacket pocket. "Thanks, Grandpa," they said, and quietly left.

Their affectionate farewell recalling happy-go-lucky moments and involving a small symbol of their memories has stayed with me.

Grandmas and grandpas of all ages

There was an aspect of the farewell to Joe that was common to many other farewells: The most tender tributes and emotional reactions at funerals are often about grandparents. Occasionally the tears of young members of the family are for the loss of a *great*-grandparent. The oldest generation that a child regularly interacts with often has an exceptional place in that person's life.

Trips to Disneyland or world travel might be mentioned in the family interview at your death, but don't count on those big events rising to the top in family memories.

Memories like these were far more common for me to hear from the families I worked with:

- *Grandpa brushed my hair every morning before I got on the school bus.*
- *Grandma and Grandpa were at every one of my ball games.*
- *Grandma sewed my dance outfits and all my Halloween costumes.*
- *We always went to Grandma and Grandpa's for Sunday dinner and holidays.*
- *My grandparents picked me up after school because my parents were at work.*

And here is my all-time favorite from an adult talking about her daughter's regard for Grandpa: "My daughter took her grandfather to school for show-and-tell." The old man himself was what that little girl wanted to show her friends.

It's the small moments that become priceless memories.

At the funeral of an elderly lady, I asked those gathered if there was a memory anyone wanted to share. A young child in the back spoke up shyly. He said that his grandma had always sung to him at night when he was going to bed. When I asked what song she sang to him, he said "You Are My Sunshine." Thank goodness I had the presence of mind to ask this child if he would like to hear that song again. He nodded, and the whole crowd sang "You Are My Sunshine"—exactly the right thing for us to do.

At the opening of another ceremony, a young man walked in from the back and reverently placed a baseball bat on the table near his grandmother's urn. This was the first bat he was given—a gift from his grandmother when he was a young boy. We lit candles around it to honor the significance of this object.

His grandparents had been in the bleachers for all his games when he was growing up—faithfully present, connecting across the field, cheering for him in every way they could. At the time of his grandmother's funeral, he was in college playing baseball. His grandparents gave him a legacy of abiding support. Bringing that bat to his grandmother's funeral said far more about honor and gratitude than words ever could.

When words fail to describe our legacy, the memory of our presence will not fail.

And hundreds of observations have led me to conclude that gratitude for a life often gravitates to small lighthearted moments that were shared.

● Ellie, eighty-three years

A legacy is created through the time we share with someone we love, especially through repeated actions. Legacy embeds in the personal ways that we showed we cared.

One of the most common ways that family members do this is through making something, such as a meal. Family gatherings of two or two hundred are frequently held around food. A humble kitchen utensil or recipe can become a symbol of love.

Ellie let her family know how much she loved them through her words of blessing and guidance, and her big hugs. She made it a habit to say, "I love you. God bless you," when she turned in for the night or when she was heading out for the day.

In addition, she was a great cook. As her family and I were preparing the service honoring Ellie, one of her sons shared that he loved hearing his mother's wedding ring clank against the tortilla roller in their kitchen when he woke up. That sound meant there would be delicious tortillas on the supper table that night.

At her funeral, family members came forward, rolled her tortilla roller in their hands, and placed a memento from Ellie's life on a table at the front. Several shared a memory as they did this. Her tortilla roller passed from one person to another with a story being shared by whomever held it. With each passage of this kitchen utensil that had been in mom's hands, the family celebrated Ellie's legacy.

● Warren, seventy-eight years

Warren met Carol in 1955, when Carol skated into Warren's arms as she was trying to get away from another boy at the

Skateland roller rink. I was delighted that those skates came to the ceremony honoring Warren's life. Carol and her daughter had kept them—a sweet symbol of the spark of love that glowed through the years.

Warren didn't have a lot of love in his childhood and neither did Carol, but they created love together and poured it on their family. Warren cultivated humor, too. He was a resilient, kind, and caring man.

If I were to write words commending to eternal rest the generations who have cared for children and grandchildren, my words would resemble what was offered by Warren's family at his memorial service. Family members contributed a line to this litany, after which everyone said, "I will remember you."*

Carol and Warren going to their prom in 1957. They married in 1958 and weren't parted until Warren's death in 2013.

Because you had strong arms to hold and protect me... and you tried to convince me that mushrooms on pizza were eyeballs [from his wife, Carol]... "I will remember you."

Because you taught me to always be kind, loyal and true . . . and because you stood

---

* This litany was adapted from the original written by Rabbis Jack Riemer and Sylvan Kamens. The rabbis might not have foreseen how their litany would evolve into personal remembrances, but it has been effectively adapted by many families.

in the camper and laughed while a baby bear got closer to eat both the potato chips and me! [from his daughter Tami] ... "I will remember you."

Because you taught me what "family" really means...and chased after me when Daisy the horse ran away with me [from his daughter Amy] ... "I will remember you."

Because you taught me how to enjoy the simple things in life... and we shared a wacky sense of humor [from Ana, like a daughter to him] ... "I will remember you."

Because you built a log cabin, played with my dolls in the doll house, and told me funny jokes to make me laugh [from his granddaughter Dani] ... "I will remember you."

Love and legacy are in little moments such as those.

Mary Lou, eighty-five years

Mary Lou brought a lot of "yes" to life. She danced through her days with a positive spirit, smiles, good food, hard work, fiery energy... and making sure everybody in the family was well-dressed and had polished shoes. She was compassionate and friendly. It was hard to go shopping in King Soopers with Mary Lou because she had a long career there and everybody knew and loved her.

Her pride and joy, her granddaughter, described Grandma Mary Lou's legacy this way. These words could go on a recipe card for a happy life:

[From Grandma I learned] to love reading, to eat chicken wings, to dance, to dress nicely and polish your shoes, to send handwritten cards, to love all God's creatures, to say, "Why not?" and jump in, to give yourself a little chocolate and Cheetos when you need it, and to have a tenacious spirit.

Bob, seventy-five years

Bob grew up between Lincoln and Osceola, Nebraska. He spent many hours of his childhood hunting and fishing with his brother and a good friend; the boys' skills were integral to putting food on the family table.

As the head of a family and a truck driver, he was prompt and orderly. Like his lunchbox, nothing in Bob's house, in his yard, or on the sidewalk in front of his house, was out of place. He was a serious and meticulous man.

He also had a big heart. Bob liked to sit in his open garage and wave to neighbors as they walked by, storyteller and courteous hub to a large community of people who all waved to Bob as they passed by.

Most of all he loved to be with his family. Bob and Mary's children, grandkids, and great-grandkids have a treasure trove of memories tied to one happy place in particular: the lake in Estes Park. That's where Bob taught three generations of his family to fish.

Bob and his wife Mary raised their grandson Zach, and a special bond grew from that. Soon after his grandfather passed away, Zach had a dream that Bob was well, sitting in a lawn chair in heaven with his friends, looking for the perfect fishing hole and trading fish stories. Zach could hear their voices. We all embraced this message that Bob was well.

When I got back in touch with the family ten years after our service honoring Bob's life, Bob's daughter Liz happily reported that the fishing tradition continues to this day, especially at Estes Park Lake. It's quite a fishing hole—they caught thirty-eight fish there a few days before my call.

One of the skills Bob taught them was how to tie a particular knot in the fishing line to secure the lure. At his funeral, the family made a big circle in front of his casket, passed a blue cord (a symbolic fishing line) around the circle, and his son Rob tied the family knot that Bob had taught them. The tradition united them in a circle of skills and, more importantly, expressed Bob's legacy of family being number one—life lessons learned at Bob's side while children, grandchildren, and great-grandchildren stood with him, waiting for a fish.

Looking like a big red jar of PowerBait, Bob wore red a lot. He was buried in his favorite red plaid jacket; the grandkids wear red plaid jackets today in remembrance of their grandpa. They know he was his family's PowerBait, gathering them all at lakeside, united and loving the moment.

Rituals—simple, accurate in detail, and personal—can bring forward a truth that is quietly held by everyone there.

ON THE TRAIL:
A SMALL PATCH OF EARTH

Whether honoring someone at their memorial service or gearing up for a challenging experience of nature, the details matter.

It's also true on the trail, as it is in the rest of life, that small moments count. There are majestic views along the Continental Divide, but majestic viewpoints have not been my favorite places. My most cherished memories are intimate moments in the mid-summer meadows.

When I enter one of those places, I want every other thought to drop out of my attention so I can look carefully, listen well, and not miss any of the small things happening around me. Summer doesn't last long in the mountains, so everything living there is busy doing what they need to do in a short period of time. Birds are singing, bees are buzzing, caterpillars are crawling, worms are doing whatever they do, butterflies are flitting, and flowers are popping out and saying in their bright colors to all the pollinators flying by, "Choose me! Choose me!" The color and activity are riotous. It is such a joyful scene.

Watching the positive, productive, committed activity down to the tiniest level makes me smile. I like to quietly sit and soak it all into myself, down to my bones. I hope that one day the remains of my bones will rest in such a place.

Fleeting moments

Some of my favorite memories on the trail lasted no more than a minute: flowers that closed before I arrived at camp, opening in the sunrise as I walked from camp in the morning. Hummingbirds attracted to a red handkerchief on my pack, buzzing so close to my shoulder that I thought they might land there. A sleepy owl woken by my passing underneath his resting spot, silently staring down at me with dark eyes. The sound of a deer munching grass four feet from my tent at sunset, unaware I was there.

Small moments connect me to something rich off the trail, too. I feel that way when family traditions and habits are reenacted: my husband preparing the goose for Christmas dinner, family laughter in response to a story that's been told many times and that we all know by heart, the simple gesture of a supportive arm around a family member's shoulder.

As Roberta knew, this is the stuff of the bounty and fullness of life. Tak for alt.

FOR READER REFLECTION

- *If a child took you to show-and-tell, what would they say about you that made an impression on the child?*

- *When the time comes, how will your family and friends complete this sentence about you: "We will remember you when we hear (or see/taste/smell/touch) _____."*

Remembering someone fondly, a grieving heart often returns to moments when the heart was light.

- *What is a lighthearted memory that a family member tells about you?*

- *What is a lighthearted memory that you have about a friend or family member, and have you told them?*

- *What are three ingredients that would be on your recipe card for a happy life? Could you find an opportunity for going around the supper table asking family how they would answer that question?*

At the next waypoint, we'll consider the value and the folly of holding onto plans.

HAVE A PLAN, THEN DROP IT

L ife stories give me a chance to consider how people have formed a better life by putting their circumstances into a bigger picture and by their willingness to adapt to new circumstances. A lengthy mesa taught me something similar: It's important to look around and adjust your perspective.

The farther I hiked on the Snow Mesa, the farther the horizon moved off in the distance. When I thought I was close to the end of the plateau, my view of the rim moved out and I realized I had farther to go. I was confused, frustrated, and concerned because a storm was coming in. But then I laughed and said, "So THIS is what is meant by 'a moving horizon!'"

The day turned out to be unlike what I had anticipated: The journey extended in time. Then extended again. And again. Snow Mesa taught me to adjust my perspective, re-energize, and move on.

Examples of adaptability in the life stories I encountered inspired me.

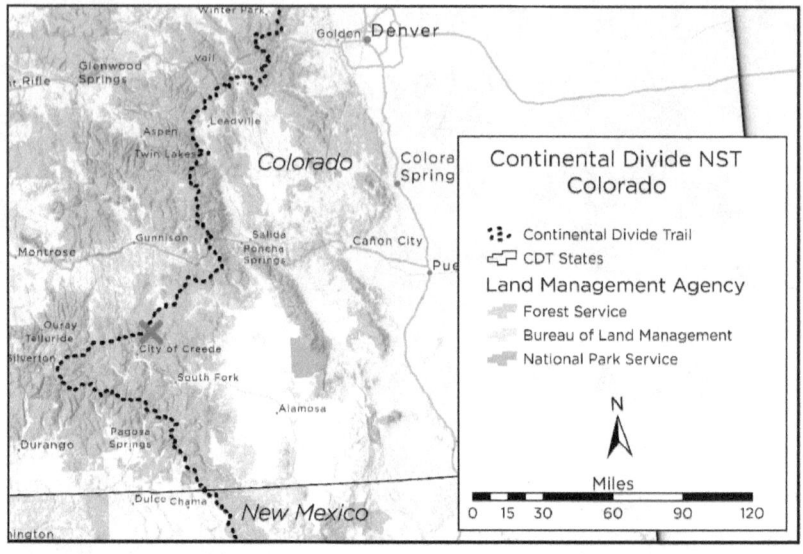

At twelve-thousand feet, Snow Mesa is the largest expanse of tundra in the lower forty-eight states.

Katharina, eighty-four years

Katharina was born in Czechoslovakia between World War I and World War II, and her childhood was profoundly influenced by the uncertainty of her older brother surviving battle. She remembered food rationing and having rations stolen. She remembered families making cakes out of coffee grounds. When a German supply convoy outside her town was attacked with bombs and machine gun fire from low-flying aircraft, townspeople risked their lives to recover supplies from the burning wreckage. With cans exploding around him, her brother picked up cans of food for his family but came home with shrapnel piercing his body. Katharina and her family were also witnesses to the worst: Nazis rounding up people and executing them en masse. How can one fathom the searing impact of these memories on a child?

When the war ended in Europe in 1945, Katharina was only thirteen years old. She married briefly and had a daughter. That marriage ended, but a second and beautiful marriage was about eight years down the road. A US soldier walked her home one day and, even though they didn't speak the same language, they somehow set up a date. It wasn't long before Katharina and Willis were married. They were devoted to each other and had a long and joyful marriage.

Katharina's strength of spirit showed in one of her favorite expressions: "Everything works out in the end and if it hasn't worked out yet, then it's not the end." In the time of suffering between two world wars and other challenges early in life, she couldn't have foreseen what was to come, but she was open to whatever came her way. Katharina was a model of resilience.

Wildflowers in the high alpine—adapting to challenging conditions and coming out of them in bloom.

Much like the garden she tended with persistent care, Katy's life started humbly and then flowered. She found a loving husband, learned a new language, bonded to the United States and became a citizen, devoted herself to her family, raised two children, and endeared herself to her grandchildren. She excelled in the domestic arts, creating a beautiful home for her family and still finding time to cultivate a lovely garden, where she spent many enjoyable hours.

● Darlene, eighty-four years

Darlene had a difficult childhood and first marriage, but throughout her life she was happy, hard-working, and treated other people kindly. She raised her children on her own before meeting her second husband, to whom she was happily married for more than forty years. Their children, nieces, and nephews commented on what a gift their example of devotion was to the family. No matter what troubles they faced, they came out the other side and kept going. She was heartbroken when her beloved passed away.

In her eighties, Darlene's final years were complicated by cancer treatment and dialysis, but she retained a positive attitude and lived a full life. Her response to illness and aging was often "I have things to do!"* which delighted her decades-younger nurses.

Her upbeat nature was tested daily, but she did not face challenges alone. Her family and friends rallied around her when she needed help, which she received with grace. Consistent with the resilience she had shown throughout her life, she faced the

---

* This is the only story that is a composite of a couple of brave people. "I have things to do" is a quote from a woman more than eighty years of age while she was in dialysis.

close of her life with a positive attitude and an inner peace that inspired her family, close friends, and passing acquaintances.

"I have things to do" might well have been her motto even as she passed from this earth.

Steven, twenty-seven years

Plans change when we want them to—and sometimes when we don't. Occasionally we drop into something so unexpected and dire that we need to be rescued. Rare is the person who has never needed rescue.

In preparing a memorial service for Stevie, I learned that he rescued people daily. He drove a tow truck. Although he was not a religious man, he had something in common with a Bible story.

When people around Jesus prodded him about what it would take to please God, Jesus gave an interesting answer. He told a story about a person who rescued somebody on the side of the road. Two other people had seen this person in need of help and had passed by, but the third person stopped. That man was a Samaritan, a bit of an outcast. He gave the first-century equivalent of a tow: He put the injured person on his donkey and took him into town where they could get help.

Today we think so highly of what this story represents that the words "good Samaritan" have made it into states' laws to protect people who pull over at the scene of an accident and help.

Helping people whose car had broken down was Stevie's job, but he was also drawn to this work because of his nature. He liked to help people. Everyone who knew Stevie said that he was compassionate, which made him excel at his work. It felt good to honor Stevie for doing this, with his tow trucks visible behind me through the chapel window.

I can't imagine how many people were glad to see Stevie pull up beside their wreck and hop down from one of those trucks to help. Figuratively speaking, there are a lot of people in this world in crumpled conditions on the side of a road. The world needs people who will tow them to safety.

ON THE TRAIL:
DIVERTED

My plan for hiking the CDT in 2021 was on the level of an expedition: My brother and I aimed to complete six hundred miles from southern Montana, through Yellowstone National Park, to the middle of northern Wyoming. (Our proposed trek is indicated by the Xs on the next map.)

This would re-connect our footsteps to where Mike and I had stopped the year before—Green River Lakes. It would be the longest hiking season I had ever tackled.

I was feeling the pressure of my age. If I was going to work through the aches and pains of an aging body and finish hiking the CDT, then I better get going. Stepping back from full-time employment made it easier to plan for things other than work, of course, and completing the CDT was at the top of my list.

Three of us were ready to embark on the 2021 hike I had in mind. I knew things might change on the trail, but I was naively hopeful that we might be close to plan.

Less than two weeks in, the stress of the hike was starting to get to us. Our third hiker got upset. This hike wasn't turning into what she had anticipated. She headed home, and I was saddened by that.

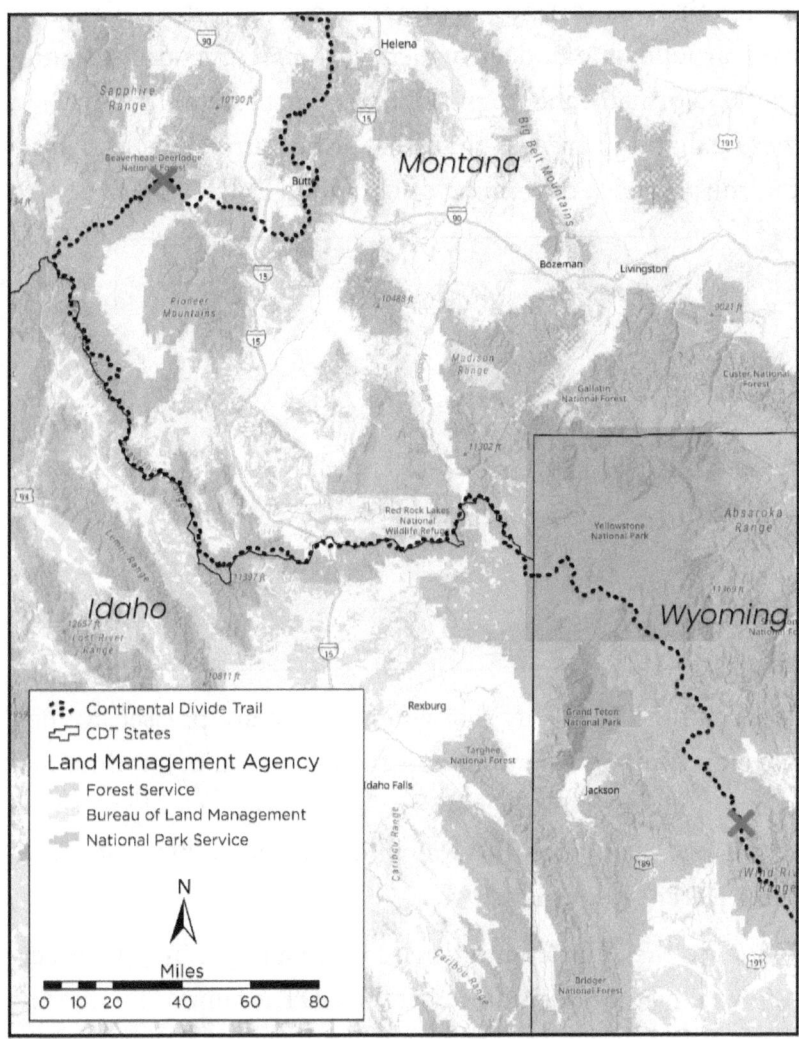

I was anxious about being the slowest of the group. Meanwhile, Mike was going through a huge adjustment in gear; he had brought too much to carry but was learning rapidly what he could pare down.

The toughest challenges, however, were not in our control: It was a hot summer, and the deadfall of trees in the Pintler Mountains was horrific—in some places even historic. Crawling over, around, and under downed trees slowed us down significantly. Normally able to put in fifteen or more miles a day, we were exhausted by less than that. And our slower pace was putting us at risk of running out of food.

I learned the hard way that when people are pressed to their physical limits, their mind isn't fully functioning, and neither is emotional perspective. We were working mightily to adjust to the trail conditions and watch out for each other, but conditions weren't in our favor.

Planning ahead for contingencies is not a bad thing; plans certainly help at the beginning. But the CDT is famous for altering plans. Our plans changed.

We skipped a 149-mile segment near the Idaho/Montana border due to our exhaustion, heat, lack of water on the trail ahead, and lack of resupply options for a hundred of those miles. That piece of land is exhausting to hike and notoriously difficult to navigate. Three days after our decision to bounce ahead, a fire came through and closed the section we would have entered the next day—confirmation that it had been a good idea to get out of there. (I returned to hike that part the following year.)

Meanwhile, adjacent to the southern border of Montana, Mike and I were on our own again. Making a fresh start in the much gentler Centennial Mountains south of Lima was great, and we made decent progress all the way through Yellowstone.

After Yellowstone, our plans changed again when we couldn't cross a flooded river. We waited for the water to go down, but the daily heavy storms had dampened more than our gear. Our energy hit a low point. It was so dang uncomfortable to crawl into a tent after hours of pelting rain and then get up and slog through mud so thick we could barely make progress. When we finally made it to our resupply point at Brooks Lake Lodge, there was another snag: I had under-packed the food box waiting for us. This was bad. We needed to go into Dubois, Wyoming, several miles away, to get more food.

I went from camp site to camp site asking if anyone could take us into town. I even offered to buy a night's lodging. Finally, a couple with a leaking camper took our offer. We all went into town, dried out, ate like kings and queens, showered, and slept like babes.

To catch up on our schedule that had us meeting my husband for a ride back to Colorado, we hitchhiked down the trail about fifty miles into the middle of the woods west of Dubois, hiked south to Green River Lakes, then hitched a ride into Pinedale with a family that took pity on us—it was raining again and we looked like drowned rodents.

This was a choppy way for us to get home, but it was safer than bulldogging through the trail conditions. Two years later,

I filled in that fifty-mile gap near Dubois. The experience was calm, peaceful, and marked by memorable encounters with people and wildlife. The logistics of coming back weren't easy, but the reboot was so worthy of the effort.

A bad idea

Plans can also change because somebody's original idea was a bad one. This mistake I made was a doozy.

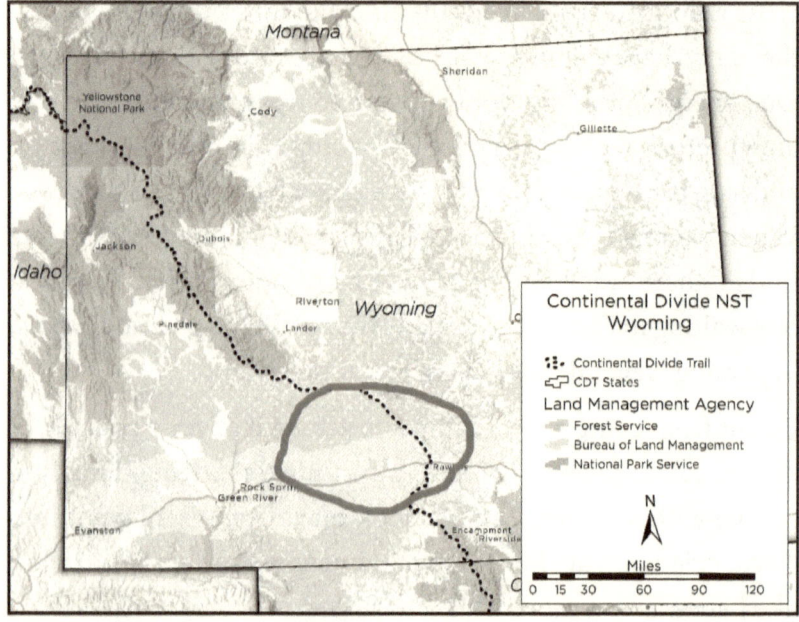

The Great Divide Basin (circled) is the name for that huge, wide-open park in the middle of southern Wyoming.

It's flat in comparison to everywhere else on the Continental Divide. It's also usually dry and quite windy; in summer, it's full of ticks. From here north, there starts to be more than a hundred miles between resupply towns. Some people say, "Geez, why go there?" Well, I loved it! Something about those big, big skies and far, far horizons drew me in.

The first time I attempted to traverse the Basin was at the end of September 2017. I was not hiking. I'd planned to cover that long distance quicker by riding a bike so I wouldn't have to carry six days of food.

This was a bad idea. I took a few practice rides, but I had never been on a long bicycle trek before. I knew how to change a tire, but not much more than that if my bike broke down. And I was by myself.

A shuttle driver took me a hundred miles from Rawlins to the tiny town of South Pass City; I was immediately off to an inauspicious start. I headed the wrong way. I rode ten miles before I caught my mistake and, feeling like an idiot, made a U-turn.

The night before big game season, there were hunters aplenty driving the roads and scoping out where they might get a pronghorn. Several cars stopped and asked if I was okay. (Did they see something I didn't?) A sheriff commented about the mud being bad, particularly at a spot I was coming to. After he left, it hit me: The place he mentioned was fifty miles down the road. Debilitating mud clung to my wheels and forced me to stop regularly so I could peel it off the tires. There was no way I was going to make it fifty miles and then slog through a deeper bog.

In addition, a storm was barreling down on me in true Wyoming fashion. In a big basin, there is nothing to stop that wind. I turned around into the storm I had been trying to keep ahead of all day. I turned around because I had crossed a cattleguard a mile back that would be a good place to camp. I began to think that I should flag down a ride to get back to the nearest town, Atlantic City. Anybody driving over that cattleguard would make a racket.

The view south from the top of the Great Divide Basin has a few more road bumps than elsewhere in the Basin. You can also see the brewing storm that chased me down the road.

That was the smartest choice I made that day. I set up my tent next to the cattleguard and fixed dinner. Shortly after sunset, I exploded out of my shelter when a truck rumbled by. Without giving any thought to this whatsoever, I ran up to the truck and shouted through the side window, "I need a ride to Atlantic City!" As soon as the words were out of my mouth, I was relieved to recognize the two men in the truck. They had passed me going the other way.

"Wait a minute. Didn't I see you guys earlier today? What happened?" They had their own small emergency. When they got to their intended campsite to set up their large walled tent, they realized they had left the tent pegs at home in the garage. Lucky for me, they were heading back to get them.

No questions asked, I disassembled my tent, and we threw my gear into the back of their truck. (I do not advise hitchhiking solo nor choosing the first people who come along with only the barest assessment.) We all squished into the front seat and headed back to Atlantic City. There was no cell coverage nearby, so I needed to reach a landline to let the shuttle driver and my husband know that I was okay—counter to the reversal they would have picked up from my GPS tracking device.

The population of metropolitan Atlantic City is thirty-seven people. By the time we got there after dark, the townsfolk were all at the bar. I know that because the whole town was dark—except the bar. I stood there sheepishly waiting for the attention of the busy bartender so I could ask to borrow a landline. He was nice and let me make two calls. When I gave the phone back, he told me that the gentleman at the end of the bar wanted to buy me a drink. There was *no way* this little lady was going to consume alcohol that night. I needed my wits to be sharper than when I got in this pickle to begin with. I solemnly requested a ginger ale, nodding my thanks to the man wearing a big Stetson.

The two nice guys in a truck drove me back to Pinedale and I treated them to dinner. The next morning, we met up for breakfast, they left to get their tent pegs, and I cleaned my bike and made the long and humbling trek home, beginning with a shuttle back to my car in Rawlins.

Never again did I set out on a bike trip.

It's okay to try something new and be a bit adventurous, but the ship I was on was going down. I'd made a poor choice and paid for it. I'm glad I got out of there before everything fell apart. I came back the next year, boots on the ground.

Rescued

After my brother and I made it to Pinedale, Wyoming, in early August 2021, we returned to Colorado. I started thinking, "With my brother already here, where else could we go before he heads home?" My imagination turned to the San Juan

Mountains—the wildest part of Colorado. Hiking there was a decision not to be made lightly.

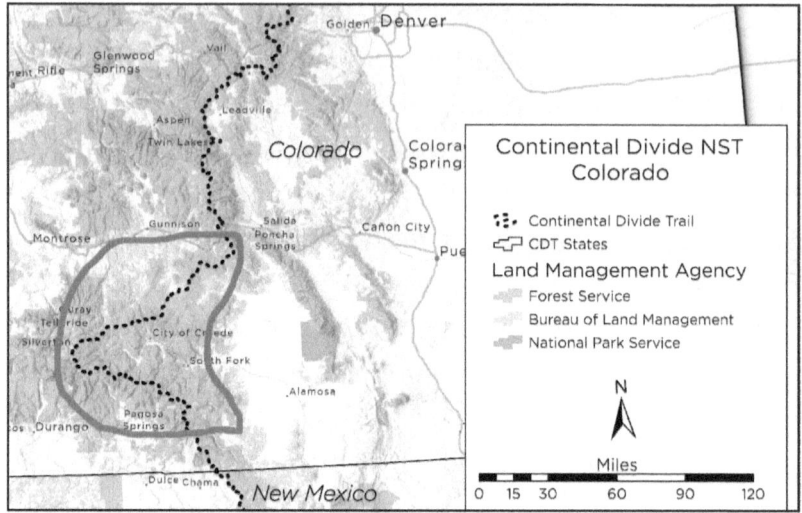

The circle roughly indicates the location of the San Juan Mountains in southwest Colorado.

The San Juans are stunningly beautiful, and they require excellent hiking skills. This is a high-elevation remote region with few easy access or escape routes. Once you are "in," there is not a quick and easy way to get "out." Furthermore, the weather is volatile and often quite gnarly—knock-you-to-the-ground-you're-not-going-anywhere gnarly. I had experienced that on a previous hike: Picture a combination of plummeting temperatures, icy snow squalls, and thunder. If I was to go there again, it would be with someone who was hearty enough to take whatever those mountains doled out. Mike and I were up for it, but our plans were about to be shredded.

My intent was to hike from Wolf Creek Pass north to the point where the CDT connects with the Colorado Trail. The junction is on top of the mountains east of the historic mining town of Silverton. After the junction on the ridgeline, completing the hike involves a dramatic drop to the Animas River where we could catch the Durango-Silverton narrow gauge train into Silverton. The train stops to pick up hikers.

A pond shortly after entering the Weminuche Wilderness in the San Juans, north of Wolf Creek Pass. Spanning almost five-hundred-thousand acres, the Weminuche is the largest wilderness area in Colorado. The CDT runs the length of it.

This was another "connect the footsteps" hike, because I had hiked all the CDT south of Wolf Creek Pass, and all the CDT north of the junction of the CDT and Colorado Trail. If I could complete this seventy-eight-mile piece north from Wolf Creek Pass to that junction of the two trails, I would have hiked all the CDT from the US/Mexico border to southern Montana. Notice I said, "I would have."

When Mike and I headed north from Wolf Creek Pass on the CDT into the Weminuche Wilderness, we were making great progress in the high terrain, much of it above ten thousand feet. Where the air is thinner and the trail is rough, hikers often don't move as quickly as they might otherwise, but we were optimistic about reaching the junction with the Colorado Trail.

On the fifth day, the rain and hail started. (I am walking in the hail stones in the photo above.) Fortunately, we were able to sit out the heaviest cloudbursts and then resume our trek.

Unfortunately, the storm persisted that night. It was hard to keep dry, especially since Mike only had a tarp for shelter rather than an enclosed tent. A rescue helicopter flew over our camp—a sign that someone else in these mountains was in trouble. We, however, were determined to hang in there and continue our journey.

But on the afternoon of the sixth day, the day we had hoped to begin our descent, the weather ambushed us. A relentless squall chased us up a ravine outside Bear Town Trailhead at Hunchback Pass (our predecessors liked creative names). We stood in our rain gear under a plastic sheet for forty-five minutes, getting colder by the minute. Soon the temperature was in the low forties. Because of the potential for hypothermia to set in, we were in a dangerous and potentially life-threatening situation. We had decent rain gear, but it was inadequate to meet the demands of a multi-hour monsoon. The San Juan Mountains are infamous for making their own micro-weather systems; we were caught in one.

In order to hike through the soaked oak brush the next morning, we covered ourselves with as much protective gear as we had available. We did not win a fashion award that day.

By God's grace or the mountain's mercy depending on how you look at it, we had stopped a couple hundred yards from an old miners' cabin. The cabin's timbers had big, open chinks between the logs, but the structure also had an intact tin roof, offering protection from the incessant rain. We made it into the cabin. If it had not been there, we would have been forced by the weather to camp at the entrance to a nearby mineshaft.

The storm lasted all night and into the next morning. We were snug in the cabin's loft, with a packrat keeping us company on the floor below. But I realized around midnight that, even if the high winds and rain stopped by sunrise, it might still be impossible for us to continue the hike. Many years before, I had hiked the trail down to the Animas River from the trail junction; the rocky narrows below the junction were probably flooded. We were also running out of food, so we couldn't hang out for a couple days waiting for this storm to subside and for the path to dry up. (Note to self: Carry extra meals.) All bets were off at this point. We needed to get off the mountain as soon as possible.

I sent a message through my GPS device to my family. When they got the message, Grete and Zach made dozens of calls to Jeep outfitters, to no avail. Because of previous bookings, there wasn't a guide available to drive to our position and get us out.

Finally, they were able to reach an outdoor store in the small town of Creede. A person associated with the store posted a plea on the town Facebook page requesting assistance for two hikers (us) who had been stranded by the storm and needed to be rescued. A good Samaritan responded. If we could get down the mountain to a pickup spot, he could get us off the mountain and into town.

We bolted from the cabin and made a beeline to the four-wheel drive road below us. Fortunately, a family that had been camping near the trailhead drove up to us on ATVs and asked if everything was okay. I replied, "No it is not. We need help."

They gave us a lift down to the meet-up location and handed us off to Robert, who took us back to his house in Creede. We dried out, Robert fed us, and he gave us warm beds. Then we discovered that Robert and my brother had attended the same small Jesuit high school in San Jose, California. We had found a haven with a delightful host, whom my brother chatted with into the night.

Robert was such a kind soul that he offered to drive us 120 miles to Durango so we could catch a return flight to Denver the next day. No doubt about it, Robert merited a trail angel award. How do you sufficiently thank a person for dropping what he was doing so he could come help us?

It's humbling to come so close to a goal and fall short of your mark. But over the course of that harrowing twenty-four hours, the mountains taught us an invaluable lesson: Sometimes walking away is the sensible choice. Further, when you do, *wherever you are*, kind people will often be there to help.

FOR READER REFLECTION

- *Are you open to unanticipated changes? Are you creative in redirecting yourself or fearful? What do you say to yourself in those moments, and do you have someone you can turn to for support through those times?*

- *What was a big change you faced in life, and how did you respond? Was there a life lesson you learned from that experience?*

- *Looking back, can you think of an experience that was painful at the time but set you on a better path?*

- *If you saw a young family member facing with fear a change they did not ask for, how would you counsel them?*

- *Did you ever find yourself in a bad situation that you needed to get out of? Were you able to do that, and what resources (including inner resources) did that involve?*

- *Did someone accompany you through that time? What did that mean to you?*

- *Is there someone whom you've been thinking about who needs your help, perhaps someone whom other people have passed by?*

At the next waypoint, we'll consider what it takes to complete long distances. "Hanging in there" is generally a more important skill than moving quickly.

PERSEVERE RATHER
THAN RACE

Long-distance hikers give high priority to speed so they can reach their goal by a particular date. Often that date looms large for good reasons: It's best to finish before the snow flies or you run out of food. Nonetheless, controlling the pressure to cover a lot of miles at break-neck speed reaps rewards.

The experience of the trail is richer if you take time to notice what's around you, take time to reflect, chat with other people on the same route, even take a few pictures to hold the memory of a good moment. Taking a bit of time to sink into the experience is energizing.

Yes, if a storm with lightning is coming in and you are exposed on a ridge, you need to get out of that situation quickly. But long-distance hiking and life are marathons more often than sprints.

Perseverance is a greater virtue than speed.

Kortnee, forty-three years

Kortnee was born and raised in Missouri along with six siblings. There was a lot of energy in a family with seven children, and Kortnee soon showed that she was up for a challenge, particularly if it involved taking care of family.

Kortnee gave birth to her first child, Devon, when she was fifteen years old. She moved to Colorado with her baby soon afterward. Determined to finish high school, she walked two miles round trip each day from daycare to school, completing her studies in 1990. Then she continued her education. She entered college, stayed focused when her second child was born, graduated with a bachelor's degree, and pursued a degree to become a registered nurse. She was also working. I'm not sure when this lady rested, but it couldn't have been often.

It was during her college days that she met the love of her life. When Kortnee married Jason, she married her best friend and was at her happiest.

What Kortnee wanted in life was simple to describe but hard to achieve: to be a good mom, to be a good wife, and to be a good neonatal intensive care nurse. Her professional accomplishments indicated unswerving dedication to expanding her knowledge of the nursing field she loved. Kortnee's family loved her, learned from her, and was inspired by her.

Kortnee took to heart the value of courageously persevering. Her reward was her family's appreciation and the satisfaction of a life that was helpful to so many people. Persisting through challenges, she spread such a good spirit into the world.

• Perry, eighty-six years

Memories from Perry's childhood include the morning of Perry's second day of kindergarten. When his mom woke him up, Perry said something like, "I went yesterday. You mean I have to go again?!" For years afterward, he would tell his family that he walked uphill both ways to and from school and without shoes on. The Great Depression in Kansas was not easy. Perry and his family would long remember the sad results of life in the Dust Bowl, with wind blowing dirt into homes through cracks in the walls.

But Perry faced childhood with an adventurous and happy spirit. Family legend included his taking a spin in the family's truck at the age of five, much to his mama's chagrin. He had a strong spirit. He survived the "dust pneumonia" prevalent in those days, and he escaped his accidental burning of the family barn while also saving his young sister.

When he was eleven years old, Perry was in a terrible accident on his family's farm in which he lost his right hand. He would correct you if you asked him how he lost his arm. "I didn't lose my arm; I lost my hand." He was insistent about that.

Perry made good use of the rest of his right arm—so good that it was common for people to not realize he was missing a hand until quite some time after meeting him. He didn't seem to need a second hand. "Five more fingernails to clip," Perry used to say. The family consensus is that when Perry got to heaven and Saint Peter offered him another hand, Perry turned it down.

When Perry passed away and his family gathered to honor him, his children said that they learned these things from their father:

To persevere through everything;

To believe in yourself;

To be kind and generous;

To fight for what you believe in.

At the beginning of our memorial service for Perry, his family entered the chapel carrying vegetables in tribute to the man who tended his family like the farm he had grown up on—with careful attention, diligence, and a light heart. His determination left his family with a legacy of wisdom.

A storm in the path, and walking through the challenges.

Betty, eighty years, and Norm, seventy-four years

Betty had a happy childhood growing up on a farm in Minnesota. She and her siblings helped with farm chores and picking the fruits and vegetables, leading to Betty's lifelong love of gardening. She left home in her late teens to live and work with a family in town and go to school. At around twenty-three, she left Minnesota to marry Norman.

In 1957, all of Norm's possessions were in the trunk of his DeSoto. When he was starting out, he worked at a body shop fixing wrecked cars. Then he ran an autobody shop on South Broadway in Denver for a while. He and Betty lived above the shop. Over time, Norm accrued a lot of parts that weren't in the wrecked portions of the vehicles that came into the shop; they retained their value. As he used the functioning parts of damaged cars to repair other vehicles, his salvage business took off. He moved the business and started his first salvage yard, with Betty at his side every step of the way. The business flourished, and their home was no longer over the shop.

The family business eventually became Colorado Auto & Parts, one of the biggest businesses of its kind in Colorado. When people sometimes called it a "junkyard," Norm always corrected them. He ran "an automotive salvage and dismantling parlor." By any name, it was a tremendous success.

Disaster struck when the terrible flood of 1965 wiped out the property. The flood moved the salvage inventory downriver off the property while simultaneously moving trash and debris onto the land from upriver. It was a mess, and the car parts were a total loss.

Betty and Norm didn't give up. Many people stepped up to help, including neighboring businesses and a friend who owned a salvage business in Greeley. Betty had a just-do-it attitude from the time she was a child. While Norm was rebuilding, she got another job to make ends meet. She was steadfast in her protection of the family business, no matter what it took.

Although Betty and Norm had a modest start to their lives, they created a strong partnership in both business and marriage. They endured. They were respected for exceptional generosity, including festive gatherings that overflowed with love. And now the admiration given to them in life endures in their legacy.

Norm preceded Betty in death. At Betty's funeral, a grandson said,

> The legacy they created is something I don't think they completely understood. They impacted so many people's lives. The number of people they employed throughout the years is amazing. The business they created could last for hundreds of years. Now they know what they did and they're happy together. I'm glad she's finally with my grandfather again. They had been inseparable. Every time I saw them, they were together. I hope to continue this business for generations to come.

Betty was buried next to Norm. A bench is at their resting place, with a beautiful view of the mountains for visitors to enjoy.

ON THE TRAIL:
GOOD CHOICES

Like Perry, Kortnee, Betty, and Norm, people who walk lengthy distances set standards and persevere. Will I hike all the trail, or will I skip some sections? What level of risk am I comfortable with? If I skip parts, will I go back to complete them, or never return?

When I skipped a big chunk of Wyoming, I knew I'd be back to finish it.

Wild horses in Wyoming.

Despite careful preparations, checking and re-checking packing lists, the latest trail reports, and weather, I'm always a bit nervous as I'm getting to the trail. It helps my nerves if I talk with a local pro. My shuttle driver, who checked the weather report in detail before picking me up in Lander, Wyoming, replied with hearty encouragement that I'd be fine. "You'll get rained on today, but nothing serious." With that encouragement, we continued to Atlantic City and a short distance beyond that to my entry point for the Great Divide Basin of Wyoming. (See map on page 84.)

I made my one-and-only previous attempt to cross the Basin eighteen months earlier by bike. That choice was a mistake. I wasn't experienced with long-distance bike travel. And when bad luck hit, I was faced with impassable mud that was a hybrid between pudding and taffy. Mud that lasted more than fifty miles. Mud that I later learned sent other bike trekkers off the trail at the same time I came off, which made me feel better about the choice to quit. The same shuttle service that dropped me off in 2017 was now taking me back into the Great Divide Basin a year later, but I'd left my bike at home. I'd learned that I would rather be on my own two feet than on wheels.

I was carrying five days of food—more than enough to get to Rawlins. I was looking forward to making more miles in a day than I can in the mountains. And I was openly peeved that the people I was going to share the shuttle with bailed because of the weather report. They had chosen a later departure time than I wanted, but they were the first to make a reservation, so their time choice prevailed. They canceled fifteen minutes before pickup, so there I was on their schedule, and they weren't even in the truck. I was ticked, but I also wondered if they made the better choice.

By noon on the trail, the skies were darkening, so I was putting on rain gear while I ate lunch. A few raindrops hit my map as I headed south for another hour or so. From under my hood, I watched the skies in front of me. I should have turned around more often. A flash behind me was followed immediately by a loud crack. I was in a small gully between two knolls, so I wasn't the highest thing around, but the distance from me to the thunderbolt was negligible. Shedding poles and backpack, I ran to sage bushes partly up the hill to my left so I wouldn't be at either the lowest or highest point. I wanted to distance myself from any metal, but not go more than fifty yards from my gear so I wouldn't lose track of it. I hunkered down in a small depression next to the sage and waited. I was pressed to that spot for one-and-a-half hours.

The storm didn't move so neither did I—except to cover my pack, grab a poncho, and retreat to my sage brush. At the last minute before leaving home, I'd thrown a bright yellow poncho into the pack—extra coverage in case a storm was more than my light rain jacket could handle. Good idea, ridiculous color. I think it was a leftover from a kids' fishing fair years earlier. In its favor, it was tightly wrapped in its package and easily packed. I looked like a big yellow bump in the Basin—a bright yellow gum drop that had dropped from Valhalla when the thunder god started hurling bolts. The rain was so relentless that my good rain pants were compromised, but at least I was covered.

I also noticed that I was calm. Damp, a bit cooler than I'd like, but calm. There wasn't reason to be calm, because the seconds between the flashes of lightning and the sound of thunder were not measurable in five-second-per-mile increments. The storm was *on* me. The wind was gale force and nonstop. The rain came in varying degrees of pelting. If the energy had been connected to a beast, the creature could hardly have been more single-minded.

Pronghorn in Wyoming.

I was completely silent, but about an hour into the experience, I heard words coming from deep inside—clear and calm words.

"Diane, what are the pronghorn doing?" Pronghorn are abundant in the Great Divide Basin, and for the most part, when they see you, they run. I couldn't imagine them running in this storm, so I replied out loud, "I guess they're hunkered down like I am." Immediately a response, "Well, they'll be okay and they're bigger than you are." I started laughing. Thunder cracks and pouring rain for more than an hour now, and under my gum-drop poncho, I laughed. It felt good.

As the storm moved a few miles away and the length between raindrops spread out, I got off the ground and picked up my gear, including the soaked map I tossed when I was startled by the first crack of thunder. I trudged slowly down the trail—stiff from having sat in the cold, curled into a ball. Silently, I crossed over two small hills before the sun started to come out. At a fence shielding a spring from intruders, I stopped, spread out clothes and gear, and re-grouped. I checked the wrinkled map, ate a snack, dried out, and took some time to get over feeling shaken and reclaim my wits. If this was all I'd go through today, I would be grateful enough. A few beams of sunlight boded well.

After forty minutes or so, in the mid-afternoon, I continued south to the next rise. By now, the sun was streaming through billowy white clouds, and meadowlarks were singing as if it were sunrise and nothing had disturbed their day. Glorious. But as I crested the hill, I stopped. For the second time, I went to the ground. This time I knelt slowly, and I wasn't calm; I was gasping.

In front of me were half a dozen wild horses, drying themselves in the sun and running. They didn't see me at first. They were racing, nipping at each other, kicking up heels. They were *playing.* I felt like I'd won a private viewing as a prize that I hadn't done much to earn.

I don't know anyone who hikes in Wyoming's Great Divide Basin who doesn't hope they'll see wild horses. They were bigger than I'd expected. Having come through the same storm that I did, they were cutting loose and having a grand time. They swiped hooves at each other with no serious intent to connect, ran around a stock tank for no apparent reason, chased each other up a hill and back down again, all the while tossing their ridiculously gorgeous manes. Their earthen colors—three varying shades of gray, a reddish brown, a speckled white, and one horse of solid black—blurred by my less-than-stellar vision, looked like the earth itself had risen into dancing dust columns. At any moment, when the wind changed, they might return to the sod they sprang from.

I had thought the paintings I'd seen of wild horses were romanticized, even a bit hokey, but those depictions weren't far off the mark. The real creatures looked so free, energized, downright robust, beautiful in their natural state—unaware of anything but themselves. I knelt on the ground for several minutes watching them.

I knew when they spotted me that they wouldn't keep company with me for long. They all stopped, staring at me with their dark eyes, nostrils flared to pick up my scent. When one of them snorted, they swished their tails and took off like a bevy of joking teens suddenly aware of a mom in the room. I was by myself again, still on my knees, whispering, "Thank you, thank you."

The older I get, I'm increasingly grateful that I can put myself in places where experiences like this might happen, where body and spirit might be challenged, stretched, and awakened to the wonder in this world. It's good to pause and be in awe.

Twenty-six hours later, I saw the first person I'd seen in two days. After greetings and checking in on things hikers check with each other about —water, where you started, where you're going—he asked, "What did you think of that storm yesterday?" I paused a moment, knowing he'd been only a few miles away and blown to bits like I was. We both shook our heads and laughed. Then I replied, "I thought it was fabulous."

Others in his group arrived. They were going on and I was not. I stopped early that night. I'd found a good spot in soft grass near a creek, shielded from the incessant Wyoming wind by a row of scrub oak. It was too good to pass by. As I settled into camp alone that evening, I thought of the hikers who bailed on the shuttle and wondered where they might be. But I didn't wonder if I'd made a good choice.

Hanging on

My standard for completing the CDT meant not skipping parts of the trail unless there was a compelling safety concern, such as a dangerous cliff face or deep snow. I never felt like I needed to test fate. I was often uncomfortable, but I tried to keep within the limits of my abilities, what I was willing to risk, and what I could escape if the unexpected happened.

The longest section that I went home to think about and then re-address *twice* was on the Montana/Idaho border.

I planned my first return trip cautiously. But as soon as I got there, something unexpected came up.

A dangerous section called The Knife Edge hugs the cliff wall on the left. My brother and I took one look at it and scrambled down the sloping embankment instead, safely crossing to the saddle on the right.

After meeting with my hiking partner and placing our resupplies along the 130-mile route that would take me eight days to complete, he let me know that he needed to get home to take care of some important matters. He could move quicker than I could, so he was going to hike ahead of me. I was going to be in grizzly bear country alone, which I had taken steps to avoid by finding a partner. My hiking partner was leaving.

So, I had a chat with myself: "Well, kiddo, you've been planning this hike for half a year. Are you going home?" If I could shift perspective to being solo for this, knowing that *some* other people would be out there, giving up and going home didn't feel like the right option. The choice in front of me was to continue hyper-aware. I gathered my wits and went down the trail by myself.

Hiking in grizzly country has special considerations and carrying bear spray is only the beginning. Other considerations include hanging your food away from camp, eating away from camp, being particularly alert to your surroundings, making noise if willows or brush close to the trail could provide cover for a grizzly, checking for sign of the animals' presence (footprints, scat, scratches on trees, upturned rocks and roots), knowing what to do if you see a grizzly and he sees you, knowing what to do if you see a grizzly and he *doesn't* see you, knowing *how* to use bear spray, and what to do if you're charged or attacked. For the next hundred-plus miles, that was all on my mind.

I weaved my way through thunderstorms for two days to get to the summit of Elk Mountain. There, I was rewarded. When I inadvertently spooked a golden eagle out of a tree, I watched this magnificent bird glide over the open space between mountain tops. Having that moment all to myself made me feel so fortunate and affirmed that the pace I'd chosen was right.

After that, the terrain turned into a gut-busting series of steep ascents and descents for several days, following four-wheel drive tracks that climbed steeply with no switchbacks. To create a rhythm for a crawling pace up the hills, I sang two verses of "Row, row, row your boat" before letting myself stop to catch my breath. This section became my model for persistence.

The elevation hovers close to nine thousand feet in this part of the CDT. About a hundred miles in, I started to feel lightheaded and off. I was tripping over small things on the trail and felt slightly nauseated. These are classic signs of elevation sickness. I also discovered that the battery charger I used the previous year wasn't going to make it through the confusing intersecting ridgelines of the Roller Coaster, when I was going to be particularly dependent on my phone's navigation app.

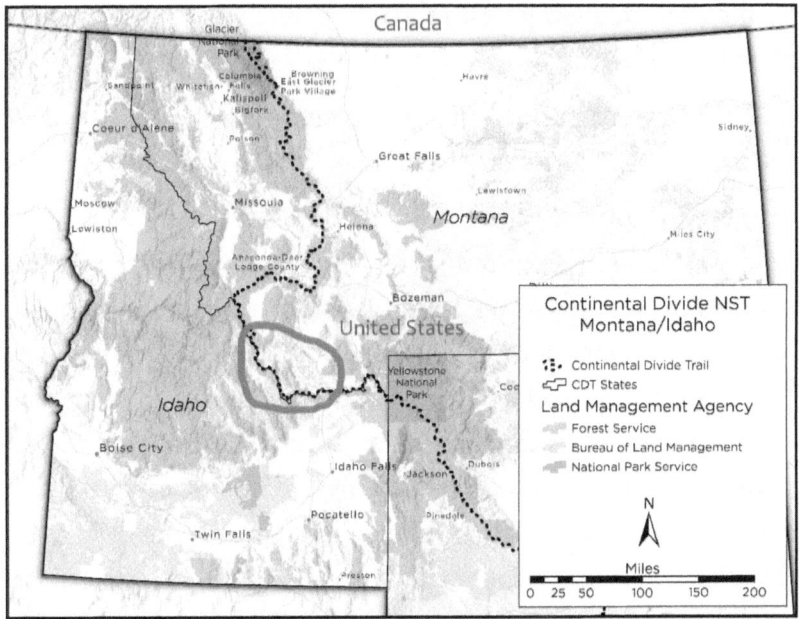

Along the border of Montana and Idaho, through Lemhi County and into the Lima Mountains—continuous ups and downs.

Ridges along what's known as the Roller Coaster.

With these considerations, I stopped at 105 miles and got a message to a trail angel and friend, Cal, who came to pick me up. "Are you okay?" he quietly asked when he got to the trail-head where I planted myself that morning. I was feeling better by then but doing my best to avoid feeling worse and needing a medical rescue.

In 2023, I went back to the final twenty-five miles, including the fourteen-mile Roller Coaster, completing it when both my physical and electronic batteries were fresh.

This was a summer of return trips to places I had previously skipped over. A few weeks later, I also re-visited the San Juan Mountains in southern Colorado to fill in the gap in the CDT when my brother and I were rescued out of there in a monsoon. I hired a guy with a four-wheel drive vehicle to bring me back to the spot where we had bolted out of a miners' cabin to get a ride. I was happy that other hikers joined me for the re-take on this part of the trail. There was a hefty rain on the night of my return, but crystal blue skies greeted us the next morning. Far back in the mountains, I filled in that .6 mile gap in the CDT, and then hiked nine miles out, down to the Animas River and the celebratory train ride that returned me to Silverton.

Reflecting on those return visits to southern Wyoming, southern Montana, and southern Colorado to complete pieces of the trail, I realized how far I'd come—not just in miles, but in attitude. Faced with disappointments and surprises, I rallied, figured out how to complete my goal, put my pack on, and kept walking.

> Hang in there. Do what you must do to reach your goal but adapt your plans when you need to. Be as careful as you can be, and don't give up.

These three efforts might have looked eccentric—even some hard-core hikers wouldn't return to a remote spot to complete such a small gap. But the hiker mantra "hike your own hike" is real for me.

Resilience on the trail was born of things I couldn't control and determination to keep going come what may. But the resilience of people I've honored in memorial services has been so much more profound. Their stories are about experiencing paths they had not chosen and reclaiming life. I am in awe of how people come through a crucible of pain and transform into someone who is strong, joyful, and full of life. I felt blessed by every occasion when I sat down and soaked up the lessons from their lives. Their stories helped me to get through times when I was exhausted. The trail was a challenge, but nothing close to what Katharina had endured in World War II, or Betty and Norm experienced when their livelihood washed away in a flood, or what Kortnee faced as a teenage mom trying to build a life. I'm in awe of these people.

On my return visit to southern Colorado in 2023, the San Juan Mountains were reflected in the window of the miners' cabin.

FOR READER REFLECTION

- *What do you aspire to become as a person relating to other people in this world? How are you training for that goal?*

- *We are spiritual as well as physical beings. If you agree, how do you take care of both aspects of yourself?*

- *"Hike your own hike" can apply to more than a physical trail. Have you ever followed standards different from the norm to get where you wanted to go? Did the experience influence how you have made other decisions for your course in life?*

- *Is there a goal you have hung onto for a very long time? Was your vision for your physical health, spirit, education, career, relationships, avocations, passions in life, or something else?*

- *Did your tenacity ever look crazy to other people or to you? Did it turn out to be worthwhile to hang in there? If so, why?*

- *Do you have a core group of people, or perhaps one special friend, cheering you on to pursue a vision that is important to you?*

At the next waypoint, we'll consider courage—what it takes to move forward in situations ripe with risk, and what it takes to live a lifetime that way.

TAKE GOOD RISKS— BE COURAGEOUS

One of my last hikes before committing myself to hiking the entire CDT was the trek from Molas Pass to Durango in southwest Colorado. I decided to hike that seventy-four-mile section of the Colorado Trail with two llamas, Red and Whalen. Our experience shaped my courage for long-distance hiking over the age of sixty.

When our trio set out, I was nervous. This was a long solo hike for me at this early point in my hiking experience, and I would be responsible for the well-being of two animals. I planned and packed carefully. I took a practice hike to remind myself what it's like to walk with llamas. And of course, I made sure I was in good physical condition, although the daily distances with grazing livestock would not be difficult.

I was as prepared as I could be, but there were memorable moments for my less-experienced self: thunderstorms less than a mile from my tent, a large wild animal sleeping fifty yards from me, plants poisonous to livestock, and more.

The biggest test was a steep, rocky descent from a narrow trail on a high cliff face heading down to a lake. There were eight hundred pounds of llama and gear behind me, a hiker and his two large barking dogs ahead of me, a steep rocky slope on my left and a sheer drop-off on the right. There was no room for maneuvering; a fall would be fatal.

I turned to the best option: Trust my team, trust my boots, trust my training, trust my gut, shout directions to the dogs' owner, and *go*. I heard the less-experienced llama humming nervously behind me. We needed to be focused, so I didn't affirm his feelings. I called back, "Dang it Whalen, you think *you're* nervous?!" We picked our steps as carefully as possible, barking dogs plastered to the hill on our left. We made it safely down the lengthy slope to the lake below, where a family watched this scene unfold. Judging by their reaction, we must have looked like I had things well in hand. They didn't hear my heart pounding.

Amazing things can happen when I am observant and ready to *go*. The trail teaches me what Anne exuded in the next story.

Courage isn't the absence of fear.
It's the willingness to walk through it to the other side.

Anne, thirty-five years

Courage takes different forms. Sometimes it rises from the depths of a person in one exceptional moment of commitment that becomes a pinnacle of their life. This is the courage of a soldier who has been preparing in body, mind, and spirit to march into a defining moment of battle.

But sometimes courage—the acceptance of risk and moving forward within that—manifests in multiple moments that span a lifetime. Brave choices made again and again to break through limits can define who you are. This is the courage that Anne had. She was born with a degenerative eye condition. By her teen years, she was almost completely blind.

Impaired vision was a limitation, but it didn't take long in Anne's presence for people to realize that she chose not to shrink in on herself in response to the challenges and uncertainties she faced. Instead, Anne continued to expand her experience of the world. Her parents said that it was inspiring that someone who was so committed to a routine that helped her to physically navigate the world, continued to push the limits in her life. She was continually moving the boundaries of her comfort.

Anne rode a tandem bike regularly with her dad; Anne was in back as the "stoker," the rear rider following the lead of the front rider. Over the years, the two of them put at least *twenty-thousand* miles on their bike. Such a beautiful testimony to their relationship as well as their physical achievement! Anne worked out in the gym early each morning. She hiked frequently, using a hiking staff and reaching for her dad's staff to discern direction and elevation. She loved the most adventurous rides at the amusement park. Once, she even did a tandem jump out of a plane. Anne worked to become an adventurous human being.

But most touching, inspiring, and almost miraculous was Anne's courage when she was with horses. As a young child, when she had some vision, Anne had an enormous fear of horses. But as an adult, she decided to overcome that fear. With the assistance of the gentle, perceptive horses at the Therapeutic Riding Center, Anne's experience went far beyond overcoming her childhood fear. Anne formed a new passion. She grew increasingly adventurous in trail riding. When sitting on one of the tallest horses in the barn, she was known to say, "When I'm up here I don't need my eyes. I have someone else seeing for me."

Although we all have restrictions on us in one way or another, many restrictions are less than what Anne faced, and not all of us respond with the determination and courage that Anne did. Anne's presence was transformative: The people around Anne were changed by her bravery. The depth of character that anyone could sense in this woman was shaped by all the risks she consciously accepted, and people responded to that.

Suzanne, a friend from a local equine program, spent a lot of time with Anne. She said this at Anne's memorial service:

> Anne taught me that *courage*—which she was full of—is not the absence of fear, but instead the willingness to walk through it to the other side.

Throughout literature, art, and myth, horses have a strong symbolic connection to spirit and freedom. Anne borrowed their freedom for a time. Our farewell honored Anne and her release from the restraints she had experienced in this life. It was as if a horse of kindred-spirit grew wings and took his good friend with him, beyond the limits, where Anne could be fully herself. I have no doubt that Anne sees now, well beyond what any of us here can imagine. And with such courage set free, she's at full gallop.

Her parents and I agreed that Anne would like this poem. It is a memorial tribute to a horse, but I adapted it to be for Anne the rider:

Free from your limits
Now run in full stride
With friends from the past
Through fields far and wide

— *From "Farewell Prayer" by Lisa M. Bakos*

Harry, ninety-three years

Trail blazers ride down many paths, and they leave their mark on all of them.

Harry, whose middle name was Floyd, had his initials, HF, on his office door. A fierce blazer of trails, he told his children that it stood for "high frequency."

At the age of twenty, he joined the US Navy. During World War II, he was stationed in the intelligence department in Washington, DC, involved with the development of what was then called a secret weapon: radar. He later taught others about this technical marvel, while also volunteering to fly missions along the Atlantic coastline searching for enemy submarines.

Harry's first business, in partnership with his younger brother, Bill, was a fix-it shop in a shack on a large piece of property. Impressed by their hard work and enthusiasm for business, their landlord offered to give them one building if they built several for him on that property. Using only do-it-yourself manuals from the public library as their guide, they built a small business strip that was the first shopping center in Denver to be set back from the street for parking. It was on this site that they took over ownership of a building and opened a hardware store. Within ten years, they had the largest chain of hardware stores in the state. They went on to become one of Colorado's biggest industrial developers.

Along the way, Harry was a generous man, helping many people to turn around their struggling businesses or to start new businesses.

He also gave a legacy of fierceness to his children, expecting them to blaze their way through life. Harry encouraged that primary attention be given to living in the here and now, fully present and with passion. His philosophy was that there are no free handouts in life, so you must stand on your own two feet and take responsibility for your life and your future. He used to tell his kids all the time that when they faced problems or challenges, they must "take the bull by the horns and wrestle it down."

Harry was also a poet, and he would pull a child onto his lap and sing. The juxtapositions can be explained by his Welsh heritage that was important to Harry. The Welsh have a lengthy, proud history of poetry and song. And fighting.

In one of his poems, Harry said that he had "an unwavering trust—life is worthwhile." This was the other side of Harry. He was open to the possibility that there is "an enormous, boundless eternal something" around us, and its presence "blesses the worthwhileness of our efforts here."

Borys, ninety-three years

Courage and vision sang out from the life and legacy of Borys. Out of more than four hundred families, his family is the only family I have worked with that told me the complete narrative of their loved one's life in unbroken chronological order. Borys's story was embedded in his family's oral tradition. Several generations had told his story aloud to each other many times before I heard it. There were excellent reasons to share this saga of perseverance.

Borys was born in 1922 in Kovel, Ukraine. His father owned a thriving butcher shop until the Bolsheviks overthrew the czar in 1917 and communism came to Ukraine. When Lenin was succeeded by Stalin, a brutal dictatorship was born. Stalin coveted the Ukrainian region, with its incredibly rich soil and hard-working population. In 1931–1932, he closed the borders to Ukraine and the Holodomor ensued—a terrible man-made famine. Borys's family survived, but the butcher shop was taken and Borys's father was forced to be a janitor at his own business.

In high school, Borys had a Jewish girlfriend. One day the Nazis came into his village, rounded up the Jews, and Borys watched as his girlfriend was marched out of town. The Jews were executed and buried in mass graves—yet another brutal outcome of tyranny.

In 1941, *every person* in Borys's high school graduating class joined the Ukrainian underground, consistent with the Ukrainian history of resistance to succumbing to a brutal overlord. They became insurgent freedom fighters. Assigned to a munitions squad, Borys and his comrades trekked through the woods undetected and sabotaged railway lines. As Hitler and Stalin were transporting supplies to troops, the insurgents blew up the tracks, took over the trains, and stole the supplies to give to their movement.

Moving west, they crossed into Poland. Not having been able to bathe or change clothes for several weeks, Borys developed a fungus in his feet and went home to recover. He planned to rejoin his squad in a few weeks, but on his way home, he was captured by the Schutzstaffel (or SS). A remarkable providence was on his side when he was detained in a town where his uncle was the mayor. When Borys was brought into the town square in the back of an open Jeep, townspeople immediately recognized him as the mayor's nephew and ran to tell the mayor that Borys had been captured. His uncle went to the SS and vouched for Borys as being "out in the woods picking berries." Because the SS knew the mayor, they let Borys go.

Borys rejoined his regiment and kept marching westward. Ending up in Germany, a few weeks before World War II came to an end, they met an American Army captain who spoke Polish, which Borys also spoke. The captain took Borys and his friends into his care and brought them to Munich.

There was a Ukrainian university in Munich. Borys was able to test out of college and begin his veterinary studies. This was a turning point in his life from which the whole world would benefit.

During school, the soup that Borys and the other students had for dinner looked like dirty laundry water, but they were grateful to have a hot meal and a roof over their heads. To support himself, Borys was paid by the brick to clean bricks lying around during the post-war rebuilding effort.

Some friends who emigrated to the United States contacted Borys and secured a sponsor for him. In 1950, Borys was on one of the last boats that left Germany for the US under a program started by former first lady Eleanor Roosevelt. He had a rough journey and was seasick during the entire voyage.

Meanwhile, Borys's family remained in Ukraine. After the war, Stalin rounded up the insurgents and their families and exiled them to Siberia for a decade. Even though they were exiled, Borys's family supported his actions; they respected that he had fought against the dictators.

When he arrived in America, Borys went through Ellis Island. As part of his sponsorship arrangements in this country, he had a train ticket to Cleveland. When he arrived at the train station in Cleveland, however, his sponsor was nowhere to be found. He wandered around with his meager belongings and $3 in his pocket. A woman working with displaced persons found him and asked if he wanted her help, but she was not a kind person. He politely declined. Instead of taking her help, Borys went up the stairs of the train station onto the streets of downtown Cleveland, alone and unable to speak English.

As he was standing at a crosswalk, a friend from Ukraine walked past him. This highly unlikely reconnection led to Borys being referred to a wonderful Ukrainian community in a small town west of Cleveland called Lorain. Borys was put in touch with a host family and participated in the church community. A family with a butcher shop gave him a job, which he deeply appreciated. Through the church, Borys also met his future wife, Stephanie. Stephanie's parents were Polish and Ukrainian immigrants, so she and Borys spoke the same languages. Stephanie, who taught English, helped Borys learn the English language.

They married in 1951 and shortly thereafter moved to Denver. By then, Borys was able to participate in a professional career again, working for Colorado Serum Company. Particularly notable was his research with alligator blood, from which he extracted cells to develop vaccines.

In 1966, Borys took a job with Norden Laboratories, a subsidiary of Smith, Kline & French. The board of directors gave Borys the extraordinary sum of $12 million—150 percent of that year's profit for the entire company—to start the research and development department.

Borys's biological division of Norden Laboratories produced the first vaccines for feline leukemia and canine parvo in addition to vaccines for rabies, distemper, and other conditions we regularly protect our pets and livestock from today.

Borys lived out the rest of his days with typical resilience. He faced other challenges, particularly when Stephanie passed away. But he kept going, lived with joy in his family, faith, companionship, and happy pursuits that included fishing whenever he could.

Borys had a remarkable life story, but despite his incredible accomplishments, he never lost his humility. And he retained his gratitude for all the blessings and opportunities that came his way. His intense work ethic was a professional legacy to colleagues and a personal legacy to his family. Everyone who knew him was inspired by his commitment to excellence.

Tested many times, Borys's happy heart and deep spirit remained strong. By virtue of personal experience as well as cultural heritage, Borys was deeply cognizant of the spiritual as well as political oppression of his country. That awareness was embedded in the traditions he embraced, including attending the Eastern Orthodox Church and raising his children in this tradition.

In observance of his roots, Borys's funeral service had traditional Ukrainian orthodox hymns, prayers, and icons, and his headstone had the wheat of Ukraine carved on it—symbol of the breadbasket that is the Ukrainian region. The tribute to his life honored his hope and determination in coming to this country. Starting a new life required depth of character, courage, and vision to persevere as he did.

ON THE TRAIL:
CROSSING THE RIVER

Completing the CDT has required me to step into courage on several occasions. Those that stand out most in my memory involved water.

At the age of four, I was washed over by a rogue wave and then hauled out of the surf by the family dog. It's my first memory. By the time I had doubled in age, other events bolstered my fear of rushing water. My first reminder of that on the CDT occurred when I hiked through the Gila River in New Mexico. Much of the route is *in* the river.

The Gila River, with me in it—crossing back and forth between its banks for more than fifty miles. This was a low water year, so the water was usually below my knees. Twice the river was up to my hips.

Halfway through the hike, I confessed my latent fear to my hiking partner, whom I had met only a few days before. "You might have mentioned that before now," he replied. We both laughed because it was a fair observation and I had been managing the river crossings without incident. I was glad that he hadn't been able to tell I was scared.

Long-distance backpacking involves facing fears. They might be rivers, wild animals, severe heights, snakes, insects, bad weather, lightning, hypothermia, running out of food, getting lost, and so many others. Four years after I navigated through the Gila River, the CDT took me across the Lewis River channel at Shoshone Lake in Yellowstone (in the next photo). It was slow, clear, and, except for coming up to my hips, unintimidating. I could handle it.

But the river crossings farther south in the Yellowstone Basin presented a special conundrum for me. I timed a hike south-bound from Montana to let those rivers go down before I got there. All that careful planning was for naught when we got to arguably the most notorious crossing in the area: the South Buffalo Fork. I heard more about this particular crossing than any other river crossing on the entire trek from Mexico to Canada.

My brother and I were within three hours of the crossing and had waded the Buffalo Fork north of this position without issue, when it started to pour. The deluge lasted forty-five minutes. We stayed in place in our rain gear and under additional cover from a tarp and trees, rather than slide down the muddy trail in the rain. In hindsight, we might have done better to continue, because when we got close to what we thought was a creek, it wasn't a creek anymore. We heard a raging river in front of us when Mike turned to me and said, "I hope we're not going to have to cross that." The sound told us it was impassable.

A flash flood filled the river channel. Two hikers were on the other side. We hailed them, and the four of us shouted intel over the sound of the raging water. We learned that "just two hours ago" the water was calmly flowing at shin level when it started to rain there. To their regret, they hunkered down in their tents rather than cross. The river was now waist-deep and torrential.

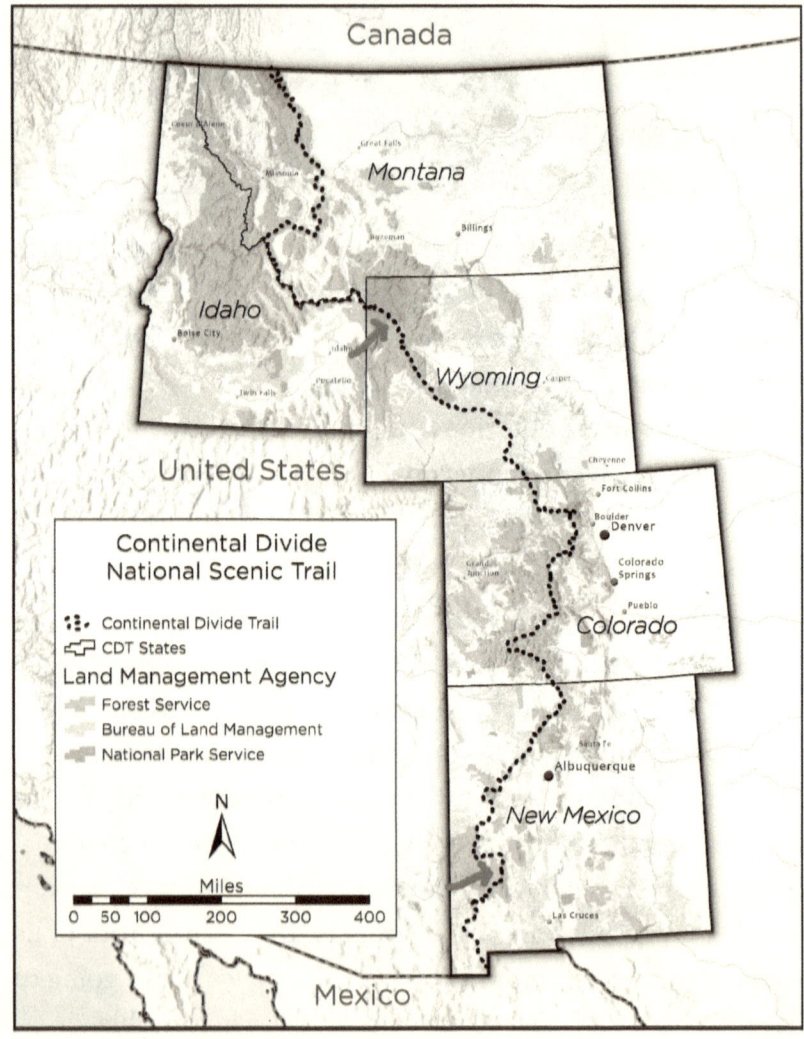

Arrows mark the Gila River area in New Mexico and, more than a thousand miles north, the Yellowstone Basin.

Meanwhile, we were drenched and running out of food. Setting up camp was a study in repurposing gear so we could stay as dry as possible through the night. We shifted tent layers, footprint, tarp, a log, and branches to create a shelter and crawl underneath, while light rain continued intermittently. We had enough food for dinner, meager supplies for breakfast, and a few snacks, but that was all. We needed to reach our resupply on the other side of the river, twelve miles away at Brooks Lake Lodge, or we'd be in trouble.

Neither of us had any idea how long it would take for a flash flood to recede, but it didn't matter whether we knew or not. The situation was what it was, and we had no options but to settle down for the night and reassess in the morning.

All night, the family's theme song for adventure ran through my dreams: the theme from *Raiders of the Lost Ark*.

We got up an hour later than usual, had breakfast, and slowly began to break camp. I kept humming my adventure theme for inspiration. Then I decided to have a little chat with the river. The water was lower but still swift. "Thank you for your effort, but we need more help," I whispered and walked back toward camp.

It wasn't long before I heard voices and the clanking of trekking poles. Four strapping young men came speedily striding down the trail, having crossed over to our side and heading north. Their presence indicated crossing the river was possible, but my mind wrestled with the physics. My body was much smaller and lighter than any of theirs. I was certain that the pack on my back was a higher percentage of my body weight, and knee-high water on them was going to be higher on me. I would be a top-heavy reed on slippery rocks in a forceful current. Mike and I waited another hour before deciding we couldn't wait any longer if we wanted to get to Brooks Lake before dark, under conditions that at the least were going to be sloppy and slow and at the worst would include more rain.

We strung our boots on top of our packs and strapped on the strong sandals we'd brought for moments like this. Mike went ahead and was halfway across before I started. I was still humming until I waded in. My first steps into the cold water sent that cheerful song slipping away like broken branches in the flood.

The river crested two inches above my knees. The bigger concerns were that it was running fast, and I couldn't see my feet because the water was laden with mud.

An old, cold, rushing fear of drowning dropped in—there was no room for error, no harbor for panic, nobody grabbing me from behind to make sure I didn't slip. There was only one option for moving forward: Face into the current, keep hold of my core, and choose my steps carefully but with purpose.

I unbuckled my hip belt and dug my poles in just enough to secure each step. Keeping three points in contact with the river bottom as I sidestepped through the waves, I chose a different song.

Barely audible over the roar, the old hymn "Guide My Feet, Lord," seeped up from years

This is how the river looked when we waded across in the morning.

of religious upbringing and a lifelong recognition of my humble status in the presence of nature. Digging into a chasm of spirit, I sang, breathed deeply, and committed.

When I joined my brother on the other side, he already had his boots on and was ready to take off down the trail. I called out, "Mike, hold on a minute." I reminded him of my history with water. When he confessed he hadn't remembered that part of my past, I was proud that he hadn't. "Give me a moment," I said. "I need to chat with the river."

Boots on, I turned back and walked to the edge, but this time I didn't have words. Instead, I gave the river a brief, wordless ritual of connection, helpful when words can't capture everything that's happened. I dug in a pole and bowed to the coursing water.

Years of ingrained feelings didn't drop away at that moment, but they changed. Rooted in experience, principles for guiding my steps solidified. Walking through challenges requires preparation. Commitment. Awareness of the situation at hand. Regard for the river doing what a river does. Honest self-assessment. Care, not folly. Core strength beyond the physical. And courage.

My ability and resolve were tested by a force as pure in its objectives as a river, a powerful fellow traveler, and we each continued our paths. I felt a tempered respect replacing an old fear. I smiled, turned, and headed down the trail. And now and then, I sang.

Like we train our body's muscles to be stronger, I found that I could train myself to be more courageous. Lives I honored in my celebrant work were a beacon showing what's possible.

FOR READER REFLECTION

- *Have you ever purposely chosen to enter a risky situation? Why did you make this choice? How did you prepare?*

- *Assuming you survived, did it change your willingness to take risks?*

- *What value do you place on courage, and how have you encouraged or discouraged it in others?*

- *Has summoning courage in one part of your life helped you to be courageous in other parts of your life?*

- *In history or in your family, is there a story of courage that you've found particularly inspiring?*

- *Does the spiritual aspect of some of these stories resonate with you, or is your reaction along the lines of, "Fine for them, but that's not me?" What role does providence have, or not have, in your perspective on your life's course?*

- *Have you overcome some old fears?*

- *As you become older and wiser, are you braver or more cautious? Why?*

At the next waypoint, we'll consider both solitude and companionship. The trail has been an experience in savoring both. Somehow, both have been connected to courage.

EMBRACE BOTH SOLITUDE AND COMPANIONSHIP

There are blessings to solitude. I hiked at least eleven hundred miles of the CDT by myself. A friend commented, "I don't like myself enough to spend that much time with just me." Not everyone likes being alone.

It does occasionally get boring, lonely, plagued by dark thoughts, but the primary concern of heading out alone is safety. As in the rest of life, going solo requires a high level of attention so that inherent risk doesn't escalate.

I circumspectly chose the sections I would hike by myself, avoiding exceptional dangers and trying to be around other hikers. My predictions were not perfect. At times I hiked for two or three days without seeing anyone else. Honestly, I loved that.

Alone, the deep quiet in wild places embraced me. Resting by a lake or in a grove of trees, I felt what it's like to just *be*, connected to the landscape and the spirit of the place but nothing else. I put down burdens and my heart filled with wonder—for nature, people I love, health, and moments of joy. I don't know all the ways that solitude on the trail affected me, but I know that it did. Recalling what my brother predicted: The trail did its work on me.

Solitude, however, was not a goal by itself. I knew I would return to community with people, and I wanted to do that refreshed so I could be present in mind and heart. The work I do assisting families is not a solitary affair.

A hiking story from my earliest days as a celebrant: When I reached the top of a long ascent in a wilderness area near Buena Vista, Colorado, the trees were old and gnarled. Decades of storms that passed through that place had shaped them.

I was unaccustomed to leading funerals, and this hike was

helping me consider this new chapter in my life. I stopped to weigh what I was facing. A still, small voice from deep inside said, "Diane, all I am asking you to do is to walk with people." I felt confidence well up inside me, because I could do that. I could walk!

Loss and grief reshape people. The walk ahead required being a companion to people in their grief. I would develop skill at this over many years, but to begin, it was helpful to think in terms of walking, something I was well acquainted with. With time, I learned that this is perhaps the greatest gift we can give to each other: to walk together, to accompany, to come alongside.

Beyond the reshaped trees was an aspen grove glittering in the early autumn sun. I don't often have the chance to see families' lives beyond grief, but I do trust that it's possible to come out the other side. I hold that hope for them.

● Malcolm, sixty-six years

As a celebrant preparing memorial services, I've carried the stories of many people whose lives included connection to nature. That connection can be a symbol for connection with people, too, and beautiful legacies are passed down from such people.

Malcolm loved his community.* His was a living recognition that we are as interconnected as the aspen groves on the mountains he loved.

---

* The story of Malcolm and Sasha is true, but names and identifying details have been changed.

As an emergency medical technician, Mal saved many lives in his mountain community. All hours of the day and night, he answered emergency calls to help someone who was hurt or lost. He and his wife, Sasha, often worked as a team. Predictably, those who lived near them said Mal and Sasha were excellent neighbors whom they were grateful for.

An aspen grove.

We are all more like aspens than we are like solo trees growing by ourselves on a lonely rock. Aspens don't start and thrive alone; they are bound together by a tight network underground. The results of their entwined roots are strong, beautiful, and resilient trees.

It's not when we're isolated that we're strong; it's when we spread ourselves around and acknowledge our connection to each other. When we break ourselves open and share who we are, that's when we have the greatest impact.

At the end of our funeral service honoring Mal, we cut aspen branches apart so that everyone could take leaves home. He would have liked that.

Jim, seventy-nine years, and DeAnn, eighty years

Perhaps you have experienced this in your own family: When two people have been partners for a lifetime, and one of them passes away, it's not unusual for the remaining partner/spouse to depart this life soon afterward. I've seen this depth of companionship in many families that I've worked with.

Jim and DeAnn were married for fifty-five years and were a team in everything they did. Their family's tributes revealed they were role models in their family. The couple gave children and grandchildren a start to life with a good head on their shoulders, sense of right and wrong, readiness to live life to its fullest, and readiness to love, to laugh, and to continue to learn. Indeed, they modeled a commitment to forming community around the children in the family.

They never envisioned life apart from each other. When DeAnn's health failed, Jim found himself planning the funeral service of his beloved. Family members could tell he was a man with a broken heart.

Within two months of DeAnn's passing, Jim was in the hospital. True to what his family called his type A personality, he'd always been high energy and highly organized; he determined the events that followed. This bolstered the family's feeling that Jim and DeAnn had a master plan all along to stay together. Even their individual wills referred only to "we." They never intended to be apart, even in death.

Jim called the family to his bedside. He was ready to see his beloved again. Their enduring companionship was the hub of everything that he and DeAnn had valued in life, and it would be at the center of their legacy once they were reunited.

Good companions in this world inspire me. I'm grateful for what they show all of us about what is possible in a relationship and how a good relationship between two people at the center of a family is good for the *entire* family.

● Ruby, seventy-eight years

A good companion didn't come into Ruby's life until she was far down the road. But oh, what a difference that made.

Ruby was born to an abusive father and a mother who was lost and perpetually tied to bad men. Born prematurely when her father threw her mother down the stairs, Ruby was rescued by her grandmother, who put tiny Ruby in a shoebox with cotton batting, placed her in front of a stove, and turned her over every hour to keep her warm. There were no neonatal intensive care units in those days.

The years that followed didn't get easier for Ruby. She accompanied her mother around the country, witnessing and, on at least one occasion, saving her mom from relationships that were physically, emotionally, and sexually abusive. Sometimes they were on their own, working in the fields to harvest fruits and crops by hand, traveling from town to town, living in cars, and bathing in rivers.

I told this difficult story at Ruby's memorial service because it put in perspective the strong, resilient, and determined person that Ruby became. It explained her pain and reserve, and it highlighted the extraordinary moments of her love for people later in life.

Ruby spent many years without moorings or compass, trying to survive the violence around her and then battling her way through the considerable ups and downs of her health. It is a testament to her persistence and religious faith that Ruby's spirit eventually headed down a path to healing.

Ruby had other meaningful long-term relationships, but with Mary, she found her deepest, truest companion. Although same-gender marriages weren't legal by Colorado law at the time, they married in a church-sanctioned ceremony. Their ceremony was at a place that had many happy memories for them—a reservoir where they had enjoyed fishing, boating, the mountain views, and gatherings with friends.

When she met Mary, the cycle of abuse in Ruby's family and loss in close relationships finally ended. Ruby and Mary shared twenty-five years together with many happy days dancing and fishing, savoring meals at a friend's restaurant, playing sports, traveling, and playing cards or (with Ruby's remarkably good luck at casinos) the slot machines in Cripple Creek.

Ruby knew something about beating the odds, after all, but I wonder if she foresaw that her life would turn around as much as it did. Releasing herself into a mutually trusting relationship with Mary, she became increasingly generous, kind, understanding, and caring. In other words, once she felt truly loved, she became her true self.

Those who knew Ruby well, wondered if she became a rock for other people—someone others could count on as a caring presence—because she had survived so much and, even as her body weakened, she was thriving as a person. As Ruby slipped into depending on Mary and others for every physical need, Mary was always at her side, true to her promise to never leave her partner in life. Ruby passed away in Mary's arms.

At the ceremony honoring Ruby's life and bringing her to her final rest, we placed a heart-shaped stone into a bowl of water. This image of a rough-edged stone coming to rest in water was a symbol of origins, tears, cleansing, blessing and peace. There before us was a visual symbol of Ruby's passage through life: A rough stone can, over many years of polishing, reveal a beautiful gem. Such was Ruby herself. A rough-hewn life had transformed into something beautiful because of a loving companion.

Ruby was a woman of quiet faith. Through all her trials, she never gave up that part of herself. At the gathering in her honor, we pictured Ruby at a lake's edge, slipping into the water as she crossed to the far shore, with ripples from her life trailing behind her. Gratitude and a deep peace surrounded all of us as we considered Ruby's story. She had found in her partner, and surely in her next adventure beyond us, the peace she had been searching for all her life: the understanding, love, and compassion of a faithful and caring companionship.

Departing, we each took home polished, sparkling red pebbles in her memory. Mary, her forever companion, sprinkled them all around her house.

Ruby's life was a story of resilience, of a life turning around from a formidable start to a life that resounded with strength and love, and how the presence of a good companion made all the difference.

Caleb, seventy years

A bear is a potent symbol of solitary strength and confidence. Complementing those qualities, it is also a symbol of protection. As evidenced by jewelry and home decor, a bear's qualities appeal to people. A bear motif has shown up at a few life celebrations, too.

I brought a small bear figurine to the funeral of a man I'll call Caleb; Caleb had wanted to go on a bear hunt in Alaska but never made it. It wasn't difficult to compare this dear man to the bear he hoped to find.

Caleb never really needed to go hunt for a bear because he *was* the family bear.

In addition to a solitary nature, bears stand for fearlessness, authority, and dominion. In those long winters when the bear is asleep, you can imagine him having thoughts that he keeps to himself. But when a bear growls, we pay attention because bears should not be trifled with. In many places, they are the top animal in the wild, so bears make the rules. They go where they want to go, big and grumbly but sensitive to whatever is happening (even underground), and they are highly protective of their children and domain.

Caleb had a perfect personality for his job in law enforcement. He was an intelligent, strong-willed, dryly humorous man, with impeccable ethics, great interest in knowing what was going on and why people did what they did, meticulous attention to detail in how something should be done, and a no-nonsense way of communicating. He was tough to talk to and he would catch *anybody* in a lie. You could not BS this man!

He was also giving and helpful—a loving pain in the a** according to his family. He was present at every grandchild's sports competition—often giving instructions from the stands. Five generations were present at the celebration of Caleb and his wife Sarah's fiftieth wedding anniversary.

When Caleb passed away, we were bringing to rest the family hero, the guy in charge, the grumbly but protective bear of his family. Sarah stroked the palm-size bear in her hands as we said our farewells.

It's not uncommon for a person to resonate with the spirit of a particular wild animal. Surely this speaks to ancient, deep connections that can only be sufficiently explained on the level of myth and lore. Deep in our cultural history and personal psychology, we carry connections to nature—reminders of the earth we came from.

Betty, ninety years, and Gus, seventy-seven years

Betty and Gus were married for a half-century. Their deaths were several years apart. In a beautiful act of uniting the memories of them, their family buried their cremated remains within the roots of a hundred-year-old tree on family ground.

Three generations gathered. Our ceremony dedicating this sacred place to the family matriarch and patriarch included these words:

Here they will rest under this old tree—symbol of the good earth that we all come from and to which we return, symbol of the passing seasons of life, and symbol of "the family tree" that has gathered to honor them and will carry their essence forward.

Here, under these summer skies, your mother, grandmother, great-grandmother; father, grandfather, and great-grandfather will rest in peace. We dedicate this simple place on family ground to every beautiful and precious memory that you have of them.

This tree is the first thing that a daughter and her husband see every morning.

When Gus and Betty's only other daughter passed away, her ashes were added to this sacred ground. The remains of loved ones now mix with ancient soil to nourish this majestic guardian of their rest. The family placed a bench at the base of the tree so that visitors could pause there for reflection.

What a wonder this is: We are each made from the same material as the earth and the stars, forever entwined.

ON THE TRAIL:
SISTER TREES

Some truths are universal. I believe *this* is: gratitude for homes that open their doors to visitors. My interviews with families in preparation for memorial services have repeatedly shown that people remember these havens of hospitality with fondness, even extending back to homes they visited in childhood.

Children gravitate to friends' homes where they feel welcome to stop by, perhaps after school, ballgame, or other event where the young people have been gathered. Kids take off their shoes, curl up on the floor, maybe lean against their host-friend and pour their heart out, or simply rest in the host's company with a cup of cocoa and a chat. If this happens a lot at a particular home, the visiting children might come to regard the adults there as extended family—additional parents or grandparents.

The impact of these memories is profound and can shape who people become.

When I'm on a long hike, sometimes I'm in places where I don't cross paths with other people for a few days. My haven of choice is a grove of trees. Trees are excellent hosts.

If a group of trees looks healthy and not in danger of toppling down on me during a windy night, I'll pitch my tent at their feet. "Sister trees" are trees that are close together and from the same generation, so they've grown up together and been through the same storms, droughts, fires, insects, and other challenges to life. According to the beautiful book *The Hidden Life of Trees* by Peter Wohlleben, they share sustenance and information with each other through their roots. They support each other with resources, warn each other of pests or drought, and function in ways that help them to keep each other alive.

When I set up my tent among such trees, I know that I'll have a good night. I can't explain why this is, but I can feel it. It's peaceful there. I cook dinner on the ground in front of them and sit on a fallen log while I eat, looking up at them. I spread my gear on the lowest branches to dry out, or I hang a water filter to fill bottles for the next day. Sometimes I say out loud what has been in my heart. I'm a verbal processer, so this lets me hear how my thoughts sound while knowing that every word will be kept in strictest confidence. One night, I cried my heart out in pain over a relationship that meant a lot to me and had gone sour. Most of the time, though, I don't say anything at all until the morning.

All night, I breathe in the good air that the trees produce. I feel warm and dry in the shelter they provide from wind and rain. If it's early summer, I wake to the cheerful burbling of a thrush on the ground nearby. (That's the best possible wake-up call, by the way.)

After breakfast and packing up, I turn to the trees. It's my custom to thank them. It seems right to express gratitude to these majestic beings for their shelter and companionship. They change me in a good way. I like to think they already knew that I was thankful.

The sergeant's friend

The ride from Augusta, Montana, to the trailhead at Benchmark Pass is almost an hour long. Twenty minutes before we reached the trailhead, three young grizzly bears—probably siblings tracking down breakfast together—ran in front of the truck I was in. They looked close to three years old, adjusting to life without Mom. We were approaching the Bob Marshall Wilderness.

My brother and I were heading back to the same trailhead where we had previously hiked north into what is affectionately called The Bob; this time, we would go south.

Packed onto the truck were about ten hikers; all were headed north except my brother and me. One was a Marine sergeant with a story. He was a rapid, sturdy hiker (no surprise there!). He organized us all on the truck (no surprise there either!). Being the oldest woman, I was ordered into the front seat.

Sarge was making good time hiking; he'd get to the Canadian border soon and complete the CDT. But he would be arriving in Canada later than planned because he had taken a break. Midway through the CDT he went to California to honor a fallen comrade. I could tell by the pain on his face that this soldier had experienced many losses; he confirmed that. He said he carried all of them in his heart while he was on the trail; he felt he owed them that.

The sergeant had paused his CDT hike to head west to that part of the Pacific Crest Trail (PCT) that a fallen comrade-in-arms had not completed. His friend had walked all but about a hundred miles of the PCT; the sergeant completed the rest for him. It was a matter of honor and fraternity. Now Sarge was back on the CDT and heading north to complete his own trail.

When we parted at the trailhead and were about to go in opposite directions, I shook his hand, thanked him for his service, and said a few words. Something simple about how honorable and good it was that he had completed the trail for his friend, and that I was sure his friend somehow knew what the sergeant had done. He didn't say a word in response, but there were tears in his eyes. He took my hand in a strong grip, nodding his head, staring deeply at me as we separated, as if he wanted to remember not just me but every face he had ever seen. And then we each went on our way. I think of him often. I still see his face.

Our paths intertwine like the threads of a rich tapestry. Nature manifests that living involves the intertwining of beings. And so, she receives anyone who carries into her wild embrace the joy and the sorrow of walking this earth.

I believe that the sacred source we came from holds our commingled and attached lives. At our best, we treat each other in ways that honor that.

Kindred souls

One of my favorite moments with Mike on the CDT was while hiking in central Montana. In the middle of a day with multiple steep ascents, we paused on a summit to rest and eat lunch. This would be a long-for-us nineteen-mile day, dashing to reach water at Rogers Pass. We looked back at all the ridges we'd climbed. Mike enthused that what we had accomplished in that section had been extraordinary: long miles despite serious elevation gain, heat, and low water resources. Then he proceeded to suggest mileage goals that were the same or greater. I looked at him like he was nuts and sputtered, "This is our new daily standard? *Extraordinary?*" We laughed and laughed.

Mike and I knew that our limits were being stretched by a landscape that required dig-down-deep effort. While Mike was an athlete all his life, I was not; that summer was probably the pinnacle of my physical abilities. Our rewards were stunning vistas and memorable moments of camaraderie with each other and with other hikers.

Mike and me heading into Yellowstone. The best partners watch out for each other.

What stood out for me was experiencing this challenge and connection with nature *together*. Even if I had been able to somehow complete the CDT alone (which wasn't a certainty), it wouldn't have been as safe, as fun, or nearly as satisfying.

On the trail or off, a good partner provides a layer of safety by checking the state of mind and decisions of the other person. We are vital to each other's well-being.

Wherever we go, traveling with kindred souls is best.

I was a trail angel for these hikers in New Mexico in April 2022, giving them food, water, and advice about the trail ahead as they moved through the desert. When we parted, I said, "Who knows, maybe I'll see you in Wyoming in August when I'm hiking with my brother."

Four months later, we met going opposite directions in northern Wyoming. We recognized each other. They even knew who Mike was.

To my surprise, they told me that they quoted me on the trail many times.

"Oh God," I thought, "What did I say?"

It turns out that what I said was good. I had told them, "Make good choices." In their long march north, they had chosen routes carefully so they all could make it. They were on their way to Canada as a team.

There is an unmistakable camaraderie on the trail, and there are times when hikers are each other's lifeline. People going in opposite directions on the same trail usually stop when they encounter each other. We give an encouraging word, tell stories from the trail, share information, and occasionally share gear—a piece of duct tape could make somebody else's torn pack whole again. Perhaps most importantly, if water sources are rare, we share intel on how to find water. I wish that sharing important information were as common elsewhere on life's path.

Creature companions

When I was away from other humans, solitary in nature, I wasn't alone. I had many companions.

I must be a tranquil sleeper, because outside Horca, Colorado, a deer bedded down within a few yards of my tent next to the Conejos River. She was so close that I could hear her breathing. We slept peacefully together all night.

In Montana, a young deer walked up to Mike and me, bobbing its head trying to figure out what we were. Such innocence! We stood still while he passed by.

My most frequent animal companions were birds. There were so many that it would be difficult to tell stories about all of them, but my favorite avian companions were the owls. Some dive-bombed our tent at night trying to figure out "whooooo" Mike and I were. I especially liked to lay in my sleeping bag at night and listen to owls calling to each other as they made their nightly rounds.

I also valued vultures. Many people don't have a kind view of these birds, because they're rather ugly and they eat dead animals. I used to occasionally look up at one circling over me and, while shaking my fist, call out, "Not yet!" But I came to respect them and appreciate their companionship.

Being in the funeral world, I was hesitant to see a connection; what a gloomy stereotype a vulture totem would be. But in some Native American cultures vultures are regarded as the animal who accompanies people on their transition to the afterlife—a necessary and respected role.

After that was pointed out to me, I saw a large flock of vultures (called a committee) perched in a tree watching me go by as I walked up a long valley. We were in each others' view for a long time. With their wings spread out to dry them, they turned their full bodies as I proceeded up the valley, shifting every few minutes so the committee faced me directly for close to an hour. As I left the valley, I turned to look at them, smiled, bowed, and said goodbye. Were they recognizing a kinship? I don't know. But I've smiled at vultures ever since.

What tale of adventure would be complete without giving a shoutout to those who could have eaten me but didn't. Lions who saw me but didn't make their presence known—thank you. And the many black bears whom I saw scurrying away when they saw me—thank you. I cherish the memory of a mama bear running across a huge meadow ahead of me with her little black speck of a cub scampering to keep up. They were in the distance, and the meadow belonged to all of us that day.

A lone swan as I walked through the Wind River Range in Wyoming. Huge and stunningly beautiful, if they fly close enough to you, you can hear the loud whoosh, whoosh of their wings.

The apex predators stand out in memory, of course. In addition to the young grizzlies that we saw near the Bob Marshall Wilderness in Montana, my brother and I saw several grizzly bear tracks when we hiked in Yellowstone and Glacier National Parks. We were always relieved if the tracks were going in the opposite direction. The cubs' tracks were bigger than my boot.

When we were about to enter a meadow in Yellowstone, we paused when two hikers coming our way told us they had been bluff charged (a charge that doesn't end with an attack). The charge had resulted from their startling a grizzly and interrupting his breakfast by shouting "Bear!" This was a dumb thing to do because the bear hadn't seen them, so they could have snuck away unnoticed. Now the problem was ours.

I asked Mike, "How long does it take a grizzly bear to eat breakfast?"

We had no idea. We waited close to an hour before cautiously proceeding down the trail, rehearsing what to do if there was an encounter. Fortunately, we saw no sign of the bruin.

Seeing wolf tracks for the first time was a moving experience. We were in the Bob Marshall Wilderness when Mike showed me how to read the prints and pick out the pack members: the male, female, and pups. Judging by the freshness of the tracks, we had slept down the hill from a small pack that had slipped by us noiselessly during the night. The male's footprint was the size of Mike's hand—much bigger than the print of any neighborhood dog.

Traveling through wild animals' home spaces taught me to be respectful in my passage: Don't be naive to danger; be aware and give them priority. With humility, each encounter becomes a gift.

Midnight on Cumbres Pass

Cumbres Pass is on the New Mexico/Colorado border. While camped there heading north, I had one of my closest encounters with a large animal. The experience left a lasting impression of a wild companion.

It was my last night on the trail from Ghost Ranch, New Mexico, to the Colorado border—a segment I dubbed "one hundred miles of up"—and I was deeply tired. I've lived with elk in my neighborhood for thirty years, so an elk bugle is unmistakable to me. I woke to an elk's bugle and realized its source was within forty yards of my tent.

It was midnight when he let out one long bellow. For the next two hours, he bugled three more times, completing his calls to the compass directions while circling around my position.

Each time he called, I woke, listened, and went back to sleep. I'd never heard of an elk trampling somebody in their tent in the middle of the night, so I didn't get up. He did nothing threatening. When I got out of my tent in the morning, he was gone.

The elk's presence could be interpreted in different ways (close to mating season, he was on the prowl), but because he never came closer or was aggressive, I think he was simply marking out his space and mine. Perhaps he was also reminding me to stay put and be quiet (which I was); I hope I earned my spot. Being encircled in the depth of night by this symbol of wildness, I felt we had accepted each other. When I left camp the next morning, I shouted "Thank you" into the wild sunrise.

Sunrise above Cumbres Pass on the southern border of Colorado.

To drop the superfluous stuff and survive on only the essentials that I carried on my back put life in perspective. The trail has helped me to see better, hear better, sense what is important, and re-shape myself to fit what I encounter. The trail also opened me up to enjoy the companionship of nature and God. Now and then I had one-of-a-kind moments that I couldn't have experienced any other way. In other words, the trail helped re-center who I am.

This transitory life is on sacred ground in sacred time, surrounded by the beautiful, the ancient, the wild.

Experiencing this returned me to a bigger view of the lives I'm called upon to honor. I see them differently, with a deeper knowledge that we're all connected—to each other and to all the earth's beings. Sleeping near an elk or putting a hand next to a wolf track or a boot on the same path as a bear print, listening to someone's survival story or a story of how they were a hero to their family or how they overcame odds to be the kind person they're remembered as—we need each other. We need to see and hear more authentically to pass through life with compassion.

FOR READER REFLECTION

- *Where have you felt gratitude in nature? Has that feeling changed you in any way—perhaps the way you felt about your place in nature?*

- *Have other people made a place feel like a home to you, and what impact did that have on you—perhaps the way you saw circumstances in your life or the way you felt connected to a community?*

- *Have animals (wild or pets) affected your frame of mind in going about your day? Is your perspective on the cycle of life and connections to "the family of things" affected by them?*

- *In spirit or personality, is there a wild animal that you feel a kinship with or that people compare you to?*

On accompanying someone:

- *Who would you walk with through their most difficult moments? Who have you already done this for, and who has done this for you? What did these moments mean to you and to the other person?*

- *How have you thanked or honored your human companions from the past? Even if they have passed away, it's never too late to acknowledge how important they were to you and to express gratitude.*

Albert Einstein understood the functioning of the universe better than most of us. He also appreciated that we were surrounded by mystery—which he credited as the inspiration for great science and great art. At the next waypoint, we'll consider the value of pausing to be in awe.

LOOK UP. WONDER. SEEK JOY.

I t takes millions of years for a glacier to push and drag rocks across the face of a mountain to scour out the bowl-shaped feature called a cirque. The top of the formation can be slick and steep. At the bottom, there is often a pile of rocks that the glacier left behind when it melted. Each time I crossed the face of a cirque, the grandeur left me speechless, imagining the powerful force that dug this rounded surface out of the earth.

The Cirque of the Towers in the Wind River Range in central Wyoming is one of the most spectacular glacial landscapes in North America. Standing at the bottom and then climbing over the top of one of the cirques (between the two pointiest peaks in the center of the next photo), I was in awe.

At the top of this magnificent bowl of sheered rock is Texas Pass. Its reputation resounds among hikers due to the brushy bushwack ascending into the cirque for those who are north-bound, and then the slippery rockslide one must navigate down the other side. It took Mike and I several hours to accomplish this formidable passage.

The next day, we paused at the top of the valley on the other side to look back. Progressing at a slow pace through such a large landscape, we had lost perspective on how much ground we had covered until we looked behind us. In the next photo, we are perched above what we had walked through; we had come from the other side of that jagged pass. This sight marked our progress and encouraged us immensely.

Looking back on that challenging landscape provided a metaphor for life: Some of what we find difficult, even devastating or ground-shifting and requiring a whole new perspective, has been experienced by others who were here before us. The ancient journey of life is difficult and will involve suffering— breaking apart is inevitable. But remembering that others have been here is a reminder that we can do this. The land itself models endurance and renewal, and so do remarkable life stories.

Joanie, seventy-seven years, and Meadhbh, born without breath

I first met Joanie's granddaughter, Heather, while I was writing Joanie's funeral ceremony. Heather and the rest of Joanie's family dove into that process, sharing memories with laughter as well as tears. Heather was only twenty-five.

One of Joanie's passions was gardening. Acknowledging her special skill with irises, a big bouquet of irises was nestled next to Joanie at her funeral. When I looked at them before the ceremony, I noticed that they were closed tight, like green and purple sticks. Why hadn't the funeral director asked the florist to replace them? But Heather, ever upbeat and seeing the good in things, wisely observed that both the irises and her grandma were ready to bloom into the fullness of a new life. At the close of the service, after we had released Joanie to her rest, Heather came up to the casket and I stood with her—wide-eyed. During her funeral, Joanie's irises had bloomed.

That was the beginning of a long friendship with Heather and her family. Following this experience with Joanie's funeral,

Heather and her dad both took the celebrant course so they could help other families. I was as proud as an auntie.

I've accompanied Heather in many ceremonies since then, adopted into a family that was creative, spiritually aware, and zany. I helped her honor a milestone when she walked out of her parents' house brandishing her new driver's license. I also led a ceremony celebrating her marriage to John with a Marvel-hero theme befitting this fun couple.

And then their landscape changed. A year after their wedding, I led the funeral service for Heather and John's first baby, Meadhbh. She did not survive birth; she was born without breath. Her name, pronounced Maeve, is the name of a legendary queen in Irish mythology known for her beauty, strength, and warrior spirit.

At the beginning of the pandemic when the size of funerals was strictly limited, a small group of us gathered, heartbroken, to honor little Meadhbh.

A stunning sunrise following the rain in Glacier National Park, northern Montana.

Some who walk across the bare landscape of such a loss, storm-tossed by grief, manage to cling to the goodness of life. That describes Heather and John, who believed this baby would always be a blessing in their lives. The essence of who they are inspired so many people. We knew light would return to their lives one day.

And it did. Five months later, with more family and friends present, a fellow celebrant and I led a ceremony honoring their first child's brief but impactful life and announcing that her little sister was on the way. Heather and John and their youngest daughter go forward now as a thriving family of three. Upon filling his new grandpa role, Heather's dad said, "I never knew a little person could bring such joy."

Amen to that returning joy, that light, and the cycle of life.

Through wind and water and ice, the landscape changes, endures, renews—and love remains. Through the deepest trials in life, we can endure, and love remains.

Judy, sixty-seven years

Sometimes we're taken by surprise by something we had little or no control over, and the best response is to stand back and let something awesome unfold. I had that experience while telling Judy's story.

Positive adjectives and sincere accolades gushed out of Judy's family members when they shared their memories of her. She was strong, caring, outgoing, and courageous. Judy was a hard-working woman who managed a housekeeping department and led her family in partnership with her caring husband Clayton (memorialized in a previous section).

Two of Judy's qualities that particularly caught my attention were her faithfulness and intentionality. Judy retained her faith in God and the goodness of life even though she lost both her parents while in her teens and her son died in an accident when he was twenty-one. In every peak and valley of life, the day-to-day and the challenging times, Judy showed up and was present for people. The depth of who she was shown brightly in how Judy lived.

Occasionally, symbols for a person's life are handed to me when I'm preparing a funeral, and that was the case for Judy. Judy collected both bells and butterflies, perfect symbols to represent her during our celebration of her life. Bells have long been connected to announcements and transitions. And butterflies have a symbolic connection to transition, including flight from this earth. This symbol predates Christian traditions and then was carried over into religious symbolism connected with Christ's resurrection.

With bells and butterflies present at her ceremony, one of her nephews gave a compelling tribute to his aunt that included this: "A butterfly is not born as the beautiful creature that we all admire, and that Judy loved. The beauty of the butterfly is realized toward the end of its life cycle." Poet Maya Angelou also famously noted that we focus on the butterfly's beauty without giving much thought to what it went through before that.

Judy struggled at the end of her life with cancer, a painful crucible for her passage. But the beauty, the life wisdom, and the calm that she left behind in her family were her glorious achievements.

In closing our ceremony honoring her, I offered this reflection:

> Judy was like a ringing bell reminding you of what's important, calling you back to what is good ... And when her time came to leave this earth, she heard the call to come home, to be together again with her son David.

Surely at the moment she left us, she became like one of those butterflies she loved—transformed from this life to her next life. *Free from the cocoon of this world,* free to enjoy God's garden and the company of all those she loved who got there before her.

When we all walked to the cemetery and brought Judy to rest next to her son, there was an affirmation of these thoughts that I did not anticipate. Inscribed on the bench next to her son's grave, and now next to Judy's, were the words I had said only minutes before and had never seen until we were all at her final resting place. "Free from the cocoon of this world." Those words had been there all those years since her son died, waiting for Judy to be there too.

Some will pass this off as coincidence, but I don't. I've heard too many families tell me about interventions after death to think that these occurrences are imagined or meaningless. I think Judy and her son were with us in some way beyond our comprehension. I think we got a sign that they were "free from the cocoon of this world" and doing fine. I think a gracious God reminded us.

What a wonder the cycle of life is—to be fully transformed in death, to emerge fully oneself, to be clothed in a beautiful spirit. I stand in awe of the cycle of life and death and renewal. Six months later, her beloved husband Clayton joined her on the other side. The bells rang, the butterflies danced, two souls rejoiced. And we all were reminded to look up from our lives and be happy for them.

A butterfly fossil appeared directly in front of me on the trail descending Park View Mountain outside Rocky Mountain National Park. I had lost the trail with a storm approaching, but when I paused to notice, I got down on my knees to study this fossil's perfection, smiling at this diversion from my tight focus on escaping the rain. The storm hit me moments later, but I was content.

Marty, eighty-two years

Marty was an adventurous, funny, engaging, beautiful, and beloved woman who paused regularly to look up and joyfully express her wild side.

I led the memorial service for her husband Tom in 2018. Sadly, midway into the following year, I was with their family to say farewell to Marty and to celebrate her life.

At the service, her daughters and granddaughters (Marty used to say that her family specialized in girls) were joined by numerous friends including members of her hiking club. They recalled her energy, her strength of body, mind, and spirit, and her devotion and care for Tom and everyone in her circle.

Stories flowed about how Marty was singular in how she lived life. She lived in a city but kept a heart for the wild. A favorite memory was her observation of a monthly ritual: At the full moon, Marty went outside, looked up, and howled.

This connection she had to the wild side of life helped me to prepare her ceremony. I researched wolf howls, and spoke words like these in our tribute to Marty:

> What better symbol for exuberance than howling at the moon? Imagine how joyful that looked, and how powerful the sound was, expressing sheer determination to love life and claim her place.
>
> But howling at the moon is a symbol for even more than that.
>
> Fortunate is the person who hears a howl at the moon.
>
> Wolves howl at the moon for specific reasons. At sunset, they gather those they have the closest connections to—their pack—so they can head out together on their adventures for the night. It's the female alpha wolf that has the most to say about the movement of the pack, so she is likely to initiate the howl. Marty—social model, counselor, leader of the fun—faced life like she was the alpha heading her troop into an adventure. Come what may, she initiated the gatherings and was *in*. Her pack happily followed Marty.
>
> The female wolf also howls at the end of the adventure. When it's time to regroup and go quietly home to rest, she initiates the howling. When she howled at the moon one last time, the adventure of Marty's life was coming to a close. Her final howl acknowledging the wild adventure of life was in her farewells. She was heading home to Tom and to other loved ones who had

passed over the horizon before she did. She was ready to go to them, receive their greeting, and rest.

You heard that last howl and gathered 'round. You knew it would be Marty's wish that we gather. And so, you honor her well. As she leaves us to rest, the simple act of gathering honors this woman's spirit so well.

Four years later, Marty's story went with me onto the trail.

ON THE TRAIL:
WOLVES

I wish Marty had been with Mike and me on our last morning on the CDT in 2022 when we were gifted with an experience that filled us with awe. It was the end of the first week in September. The previous night was so cold that we woke to ice on the flaps of the tent; the ice was so hard that you could knock on the door! It was funny. Sort of. A few days before, I suggested we wait an additional day to finish hiking for the year because I thought the temperatures might cool down from the upper eighties that we'd been experiencing. Well, they did. The temps dropped fifty degrees in one night. Geez! We got up that morning well before sunrise and decided (uncharacteristically) to start hiking without breakfast so we could warm up.

When sunlight reached us, we stopped. I wanted to take a picture of the beautiful markings in the frost on the fallen trees that we were clambering over. The tiny carvings looked like a form of writing. I knew they were the tracks of worms, but they looked like ancient script. The engravings were gorgeous, mysterious, and strangely moving. It was hard to stop in the cold, but I knew if I didn't, I would regret not pausing to capture this moment.

I was glad I paused to behold such beauty on a common log.

As soon as I had pictures of the worms' handiwork, I heard a sound coming from the ravine next to us.

Wolves. First there was a long, haunting howl from the leader. I'd heard coyotes howl many times, but this was notably different from a coyote howl. Around sunset, coyotes sound to me like they're getting everybody together for a party. Or if it's at sunrise, the alpha animal's howl sounds like a mom or dad telling all the kids to be quiet and go to bed. A coyote pack frequently sounds raucous. This wasn't that. It was a deeper, fuller, and somehow wilder and lonelier sound. It was also more robust than the Mexican gray wolves' howls in New Mexico. Gray wolves in the northern Rockies are larger than their Mexican cousins, and their howls reflect that.

Sunrise marks the end of the hunt. I don't know if this wolf pack was successful, but their howls sounded almost mournful. To me, the alpha's long, big, lonely howl also sounded old and deeply rooted in the place. It's difficult to explain the effect of a howl like this, but wolf howls humble me while also expanding my kinship with wild beings.

I looked at my brother. We were frozen where we stood, and not because we were cold. The second time the alpha howled, the group was closer to each other; the pack's howls were less dispersed. We turned from looking at each other to looking in the direction of the wolves, and we both smiled. Tears welled up in my eyes. I looked down, catching my breath. Without words I could tell that my brother and I were thinking the same thing. What a gift this moment was.

Worm script in the frost—looking ancient and, to quote author Cole Arthur Riley, "illegibly spiritual."* Many spiritual traditions teach awareness of the sacred in things large and small. The nineteenth-century rabbi Malbim refers to "hidden miracles;" he would have approved of Riley's observation.

By the alpha's third howl and the answering howls of the pack, the yips and howls were in one spot. The night's hunt was over, they had gathered, and it was time to rest. After the third chorus, silence.

Mike and I said some obvious words in response. "Do you believe that!? Oh my God, that was amazing!" We sat down. We unpacked breakfast. And while we ate facing the sun, with the warmth increasing, our words flowed.

> *We put ourselves in wild places hoping something like this will happen. There are no guarantees that it will, but oh, what a gift when it does.*

After more than five hundred miles into a summer of backpacking, the farewell to the trail was shared with wolves. We went home with the wonder and joy of that moment holding

---

* It's possible to experience wonder in the mundane. "To encounter the holy in the ordinary is to find God in the liminal—in spaces where we might subconsciously exclude it, including the sensory moments that are often illegibly spiritual." — Cole Arthur Riley.

us. If dear Marty had been with us, I'm sure she would have led us in a good howl.

The last sunrise on the trail in 2022.

It has been good for me to remember that things worthy of wonder include mountaintops and wolves, but also the "illegibly spiritual" or "hidden miracles" of worm script on fallen logs. One of my favorite historic figures, Francis of Assisi, wrote about seeing God in wolves and worms. I'm in excellent company!

So much in common experiences is worthy of marvel—the way my body heals even in old age or signals its frailty, the face of my adult daughter as she passes through life's challenges, the face of a young child who knows nothing of the world's cares and dances with abandon, and the face of an elder who has seen many of life's woes but readily embraces the child and dances.

Marty didn't have to climb a peak to howl, or circumnavigate a cirque, or hike along the spine of the continent. She walked into her front yard and looked up. Wonder is accessible.

More than the grand beauties of our lives, wonder is about having the presence to pay attention to the commonplace.

*It could be said that to find beauty in the ordinary is a
deeper exercise than climbing to the mountaintop.*

—Cole Arthur Riley

*At Upper Seymour Lake in Montana, my brother commented,
"Those photons traveled ninety-three-million miles from the
sun to strike the lake at exactly the moment you are here to see
them." I was reminded to be in awe.*

White hawks

There are moments to stand down in the presence of something bigger than oneself—to respond to the call to be present, let unfold what would unfold, and bear witness in awe. That has happened on the trail, at ceremonies, and, sometimes, in a connection of both.

In September 2020, I took a break from working on memorial services during the pandemic. I went for a long walk.

To hike from Wolf Creek Pass to Cumbres Pass in southern Colorado, I chose the less challenging but beautiful lower route—sixty-seven miles from Wolf Creek ski area down to Elwood Pass, then along the Cumbres River through the small towns of Platoro and Horca, followed by the ascent to Cumbres

Pass. I was hiking solo, but not alone. As has happened before, wild animals accompanied me.

Multiple times during this hike I looked up and saw red-tailed hawks. As I watched them circle above me with the bright September sun shining through their wings, they looked dazzling white. Again and again, they reeled in circles above me, alone or in pairs. These are not rare birds, but after seeing their striking appearance so frequently, I commented about it to other hikers.

As I was driving home afterward, I got a message that a family needed my help with a memorial service for their son. I asked his name, and when I got home, I looked up its meaning. It is a variation of a medieval name meaning "white hawk." Another meaning is "sent by God."

I don't think this was a coincidence. It's possible to go through life oblivious to deeper messages and meanings, but what a loss that would be, what a diminishment of life's heart-opening opportunities. I think my experience of the birds over me on the trail connected me to what was going on elsewhere with a grieving family.

The moment I heard his name, I pictured the circling hawks like messengers conveying what any caring community would want to say to grieving parents, encircling them and letting them know they were not alone in their grief. It has been my role and honor to encircle those who grieve.

The dance of land and sky

The landscape of a wild earth has perpetually experienced loss and trauma. Storms, fires—those events we call natural disasters shape an area's appearance. But the same landscape also has the capacity to regenerate, even to achieve natural glory—grasses and forbs move in, wildflowers bloom in colorful displays attracting pollinators that help the entire system to flourish, magnificent trees reappear given enough time. Nature manifests images of both loss and recovery, sorrow and joy.

To watch a thunderhead gather along the Continental Divide, hunker down in a grove of trees while hail hammers the ground nearby, watch clouds in misty form rush through the notch between mountains, laugh at the clouds circling a peak as if they are about to chase me down, then shiver in the cold when the storm is on me and I know the rain is not going to stop anytime soon. On and on the mountains and the clouds shape each other and I am there as witness. How fortunate I have been to watch mountains and clouds. I believe they dance.

Being fully entwined in life's cycles means there will be times of breaking apart. It can be hard to accept, but breaking down might need to happen before we can grow to all we can be. What a mystery it is, to dance through any landscape or storm.

FOR READER REFLECTION

- *Have you looked back lately and reviewed where you've come from and what you've crossed through? Be encouraged. Even when grief and suffering strip you, you can come through. You can grow. You can gain new insights into yourself, into those you love, into life itself. Do you see the possibility of even becoming a beacon to others?*

- *How have you experienced mystery? Have you stopped in awe and marveled at what you saw or heard?*

- *Are there times in your life when you feel you have been visited by a person or something in nature that has a message for you? Did that change your perspective in any way? Do you feel that was a good thing, or crazy, or —?*

- *Have there been times in your life when you felt like something bigger than you was watching out for you?*

- *Have there been low times when you purposely sought out some-thing you knew would bring you joy? Did joy find you?*

At the next waypoint, we'll consider the fluidity of time and what that does to our perspective.

Witness to a wonder, dining with a Yellowstone geyser.

REMEMBER THAT
TIME IS ENDLESS

E ven physicists have trouble defining time. Sometimes we shouldn't.

Climbing a pass in Montana, Mike and I talked about family. The hike had been long and hot, and finding water had been difficult. When the shade of trees provided a respite, we paused to rest. A single-engine plane passed overhead.

I looked up, waved, and said, "We're okay, Dad!"

Our father passed away many years ago. My hailing the plane was a salute to memory. Dad had occasionally flown his small plane in the mountains to find Mike on one of his adventures, wave the wings to let his oldest son know he'd been spotted, and then drop supplies where Mike could get to them.

I was co-pilot on one of those trips with Dad, flying over a remote section of forest on the coast of central California. I had made the granola mix, poured it into empty jugs, attached a streamer, and out the window it went. Mike saw us, retrieved the food, and was happy to get the resupply.

If he were still with us, Dad would have checked up on my brother and me to be sure we were ok. We smiled at the thought, creating a new memory of something that could have happened.

Deep in nature, memory and current experience merge.

Hiking has helped me to experience the fluidity of time the way my Celtic ancestors did, putting people at events far outside what was possible in Chronos time, measured by the calendar and clock. But spiritual time is Kairos time. Who's to say that Dad isn't still checking up on us, waving, sending spiritual supplies to keep us going? I carry forward his care for us. He's still here.

Yes, I'm aware that I must get to a resupply point. But when I'm in the presence of a glacier, or walking a mesa, or crossing a river, or picking my way down a canyon, or climbing up a valley to get to a campsite, I'm also carrying memories into these places. I'm in a different frame of mind: Aware of the present moment, I'm also steeped in the ancient. From what I've read about mysticism across the world's religions, this awareness verges on the mystical.

This dual awareness surfaces in ceremonies as well.

• Ed, sixty-five years

Growing up outdoors was a multi-generational tradition in Ed's family, a tradition that he made a point of passing on to his own children—all girls. They recall fishing, canoeing, "Jeeping," and camping with their father and extended family—all over the mountains of Colorado. He wanted his children to push themselves physically and intellectually—taking on intellectual development like pushing to the summit of a mountain—with the goal of taking in all that life could include. He didn't give trinkets to his daughters; he gave them an atlas and a base-ball glove. Applying the skills he learned while apprenticed to a shipwright, Ed and his children worked together to build a canoe. The result was a family treasure.

Ed was also a man who had endured heartaches. His mother died when he was ten years old. When he was an adult, one of his three daughters passed away. Ed struggled with health problems and had difficulty getting around, unfortunately. He died when he was only sixty-five.

Our memorial tribute to Ed acknowledged that he and the daughter he lost had shared Buddhist beliefs: that we each have a soul, and that at death, the soul leaves the body and moves on. We rang a singing bowl to mark the departure of Ed's soul as it traveled to rejoin the soul of his daughter. What a poignant reunion that must have been. They had waited a long time to get together.

The Book of Ecclesiastes in Hebrew scriptures (the Old Testament in the Christian Bible) provides an example of Kairos time, which some call God's time. It refers to experiencing time as opportune moments or seasons of something coming to fruition. We read this in Ed's service.

> To everything there is a season, and a time to every purpose under the heaven:
>
> A time to be born, and a time to die;
>
> A time to weep, and a time to laugh;
>
> A time to mourn, and a time to dance.

While Ed embarked on his journey to see a child he had long been separated from, time also made Ed a grandfather again. Two days before his funeral, his third grandchild was born—a baby girl. In the mystery of the cycle of life, a child came into the world as we were saying goodbye to her grandfather. The first public pronouncement of the baby's name was made at the celebration of her grandfather's life, and we rang the bowl again.

For centuries and across cultures, bells have signified the passage of time and a soul's change. The bell-like sound of a singing bowl is said to match a sound in the universe. Perhaps this is related to the vibration of the planets, each sounding its own tone. It's wonderful to imagine the planets singing!

Among his many skills, Ed was a weaver. Like one of his weavings, the beauty of a pattern might not be visible while the weaving was incomplete. But when the weaving is finished and turned over, the final image shows the joy woven into the pattern.

We returned him to the mountains and rivers, to the dust of the stars whence we all come. Ed's sister read a poem about a fisherman in the mists, mountains, and clear water, from the wilderness poetry tradition of ancient China.

In Ed's journey, a joyful pattern emerged out of sadness—in how he took on life, in how he led his daughters to be adventurous and strong, and then in death. With the departure of one soul, another wound her way through the universe and arrived. One day, Ed's family would tell this child that she appeared under the watchful star of her grandfather.

Alice, eighty-nine years

Of the hundreds of family members I have interviewed while preparing ceremonies marking significant life events, a handful of relationships with families have lasted several years. Alice's family was one of those I had the honor to accompany more than once. I presented two ceremonies for them in a decade— one celebrating the life of Alice's son and then one celebrating Alice.

Alice was an adventurous soul, quite comfortable outdoors. This especially showed in her lifelong kinship with water. For example, to pursue her passion for fishing, Alice embraced standing in streams. Her soulmate in this passion was her husband Dale. Most of their adventures and many highlights of family life happened in or next to rivers.

Alice and Dale raised two children, a daughter and a son. Alice's simple priorities and bighearted, down-to-earth nature showed in her devotion to their family. When they realized that their infant son Jimmy was deaf, they quickly moved the family to Denver so that Jimmy could go to schools that taught deaf children. Alice learned sign language to communicate with her son and dedicated herself to doing everything she possibly could to prepare Jimmy for an independent and successful life.

Once their children were on their own, Alice and Dale retired to the small town of Howard, Colorado, to enjoy simple pleasures. They loved their home in a cabin by a creek that ran into the Arkansas River. With easy access to fishing and hiking, Alice especially loved being at a river with their kids, grandkids, great-grandkids, friends, and neighbors. A few steps from her front door, the waters of the creek coursed through her days.

She liked to sit on her porch, listen to the stream, and walk along the waters' edge. And like the water she spent a lot of time with, she was the calm, caring presence as life flowed by.

In her quiet way, Alice became a matriarch of the small town of Howard. People from all around stopped by to sit on her porch, chat with Alice, and have a cup of coffee after their morning walk. The lady up the hill would start out walking with her dog, then pick up Alice and her dog Bo, and they continued down the road picking up friends and dogs along the way. Alice hosted a weekly happy hour on her porch. Grandchildren and then great-grandchildren came to the cabin to enjoy hiking and fishing along the river with Alice and Dale. Alice was the centerpiece of every family and neighborhood gathering, accompanied by the creek she loved.

Like the chiseled banks of a channel that had floods pound through, Alice's life was not without painful losses. Both her husband and her son passed away before her, as well as her parents and siblings. Such deep loss has a profound impact on whomever bears it; the course of life isn't the same afterward.

I was with Alice's family for Jimmy's funeral before accompanying them when Alice passed away; I saw this family up close over time. I marveled at their peace. Alice's example taught them well.

In the last year of her life, Alice expressed an interest in knowing God better. She felt there was no hope in humanity all by itself, so she placed her hope in something bigger than herself. She continued to live a simple, pure, and kind life, shining more and more. Her granddaughter observed that her grandmother in her final years "had the face of Jesus."

To the end, Alice continued to stand in the river of her family's life, embracing their currents. She lived it, loved it, laughed in it. Like a rock for the people she loved, she was someone solid whom you could sit with, confide in, laugh with, and count on.

After she passed away, the family rock everyone had depended

upon for years had been removed, so it seemed more appropriate to think of Alice as the river itself. The essence of Alice flowed on to her next adventure, returning to all who got to the far shore long ago and were there to greet her. The river of Alice's life had reached its rest.

A granddaughter kept the cabin in the family; there were too many memories there to let that special place slip away. At the celebration of Alice's life, I read a poem that particularly suited her, but could describe life for any of us:

Down This River
By Trisha C. York

It's a long, long way down this river
Made of snow and rain and tears.
I am rushing along night and day
Moving even in my dreams,
Singing my water song.
Rippled laughter smoothes the stones
In the bed of my heart.

Brilliance pools within me,
Guides me through the watery shadows
Where I find what I thought was lost.

Sometimes I don't know where I'm going.
I only know the moon pulls me on this ancient path.

And just when I thought I had come to the end of me,
I am carried to the endless sea
As far as the sun can reach,
As deep as the heavens,
As blue as angel eyes.

It's a long, long way down this river
That shimmers,
And answers,
And carries,
Searching for the sea like a living prayer.

Alice dedicated herself to the flow of life.

And such a legacy she left—flowing from her life like the tributary of a living prayer.

ON THE TRAIL:
IN RIVERS

Whether you hike or not, metaphors in nature can speak to all of us. She is a well of wisdom.

One of my favorite places for reflection is a river. I've faced my fears in crossing them, but perhaps that's part of the attraction: Rivers are powerful, beautiful, and completely neutral about my presence. They simply are. They have a lot to tell me about going through life.

At the beginning of hiking season in 2018, I listened to a speaker at Trail Days in Silver City, New Mexico, giving a roomful of us hikers advice about desert hiking. "When you're hot in the desert and there's a river nearby, don't stay hot. Get in the river!" Memorable words. Get in the river. When you're depleted and in need of a resource that's right next to you, don't stumble along feeling depleted—jump in! Sit there for a while. Cool down. Soak it up. A few days later, after a long, hot hike in desert country, I remembered her words and took her advice.

My campsite along this tributary to the Gila River was far from towns and highways. The next morning, I walked down the trail into the water and hiked up the riverbed.

Walking along rivers and considering a life like Alice's reminds me that *life* is a river of events. Why not jump in? The anticipated and the surprises swirl together and move on. Standing strong in the middle are family and friends, helping us to keep our footing.

As we reached Canada, Mike and I crossed the last river beneath the watch of sister trees.

Looking back, I remember standing in the waters enjoying each other's presence, glad to be accompanied, grateful for the companionship that replenished me. I was honored to be with a brother in the river.

Like time spent with nature, death, memory, grief, and the continuance of a legacy have a fluid timeline: The present merges with what humans have experienced throughout the ages.

If we quiet ourselves and listen attentively, we'll hear in blessed memory those who passed this way before us. What would they have us see? What would they want us to carry forward?

We might share moments of raucous laughter with them, moments when troubles rush around us and we reach for support, moments of wise advice or compassionate silence, and moments of simply being, letting the currents in life slide by.

In a way we can't explain but can feel at our core, current time, memory, and events beyond our lifetime converge. Our heart opens to the sacred nature of everything around us. Common life resonates with a holy and eternal song that even the stars are singing.

Public theologian Nadia Bolz-Weber, known for thinking outside a traditional religious box, shares this perspective on the ever-unfurling story of who we are:

> ... I've had an image [of the afterlife] in my head all week—and it wasn't mansions and gold streets in heaven like in the Gospel hymns I grew up singing.... all week I've had this image of the miracle demanded by we who must die. It is the souls of the dead woven together in the presence of God, their names being spoken in pure love by God, every tear being wiped

dry, every illusion of their separateness and divisions being vanished, woven through eternity... maybe in some unfathomably spiritual sense—maybe it is the fabric of the universe itself.... We are God's children now; what we will be has not yet been revealed.

To walk in nature and to walk with the bereaved is to witness the story of the eternal and sacred, the story of ongoing creation, and the story of our place in it. This story continues to unfold, continues to reveal who we are, infused with holiness.

In his book *American Ramble*, Neil King considers that our purpose of being might be to bear witness in a fundamental way—to marvel at the wonders around us and to be kind. He had the crystalline perspective of a man fighting cancer and whose remaining time walking the earth was short. He went out on a long walk through the heart of America's historical common ground. One of the people he meets on his ramble parallels these ponderings by suggesting we are here to reflect

God's image. When I heard something like that perspective in catechism class as a little Catholic kid, it didn't make any sense to me. But now it does. After a lengthy walk, now it does.

While I walked in nature over many years, human experience and natural landscape became inextricably linked. Creation continues to create. Love is inherent in the earth's determined creativity and renewal, and in the lives of those who press forward and press in on each other in our uniquely messy but determined and also caring way. At the heart of it all is a swirling, shaping love that will find us when we're looking for it and sometimes when we're not. And that love will hold us.

Peace, be still.

Floating on Mokowanis Lake in Glacier National Park, near the end of my odyssey along the Continental Divide. All the years of hiking this trail, of carrying stories and trying to hold the connections and sacredness of it all—floated into this place of rest like a living prayer.

FOR READER REFLECTION

- *For the purpose of this reflection, I invite you to think of home as a peaceful place where you are your true self, finally revealed, loved, with grace having rubbed off any rough edges and pain. If life can be a continuing revelation of that self, how are you heading home to the best you can be?*

- *Who has stood in the river of your life? How did they accompany you? What do you carry forward from that experience?*

- *Does the river of your life include spiritual insights? How would you describe those? By what experiences/practices did they enter your life?*

- *Does a life that is "a living prayer" resonate with you? If so, what does it look like?*

REACHING THE SUMMIT

The End of the Trail

My final steps on the Continental Divide Trail led to the US/Canada border at Waterton Lake, accompanied by family members Mike, Grete and Zach. There is a monument there to mark the northern terminus of the trail, but on August 28, 2023, it represented more than that. This was the physical and emotional summit of my odyssey.

Hearing life stories gave me a touchstone to spiritual lessons—ways to open my senses, my abilities, and my heart—and the trail reinforced those. Desert and flood, rock and river, parched earth and springs, desolation and verdant richness are all part of the experience on the trail and in life. Combined with the natural wonder found along the Continental Divide, I am blessed with gratitude.

My family made sure I took a celebratory leap into the cooling waters. My husband Bob met us in Waterton Village to honor the completion of the thirty-one hundred miles that I walked over more than seven years.

The Path Forward

After reaching the endpoint of a long trail, the hiker usually goes home. A transformative experience, however, has no end. The journey folds into who we are—like a new and essential ingredient in the composition of our soul. My pilgrimage seeking the sacred elements shared by so many lives and manifest in nature has been stirred into who I am.

Now that I've completed my pilgrimage on the trail, I am expanding my world as a trail angel. I've graduated seventeen inches—from sleeping on the ground to sleeping in a small trailer, perfect for traveling to trailheads. In the hiking season that followed, I spent nine weeks assisting travelers from New Mexico to the Canadian border.

Life on the trail is a microcosm of pain and exhilaration, losses and victories, emergencies and rescues, tears and laughter. I was overwhelmed by the richness of it all.

On the horizon, a tenth waypoint emerges: *kindness*, transforming all those who give and those who receive. As in my work as a celebrant, I hope to craft a legacy that is helpful to those coming up the path. We all have this ability. Here is what I have learned.

The Waypoints That Shape Your Legacy

- *Set your eyes on what helps you thrive as a person, and then get out there. Whether your body is able or is restricted, walk in spirit.*
- *Travel lightly. Release old baggage. Experience what has roots nobody can pull up: the divine, the sacred, Spirit, God, whatever word you apply to the eternal and holy.*
- *Cherish the little moments when immense goodness shows up, including when it shows up in you. These revealing moments will be your legacy.*
- *Accept change. Plan for your well-being, but adapt, shift your horizon, and move on.*
- *Persevere. Life is a marathon more often than a sprint. Hang on. Pursue what matters.*
- *Be courageous. The best way to overcome fear is to keep moving forward.*

- *Accompany people through the highs and lows of life and let them do the same for you. We have strength and grace within us, to share and to receive.*
- *Look back and look up. Reflect on the goodness within how far you've come and lift your eyes from your footsteps. Be amazed by the wonders in this world and in this life.*
- *Listen for the river song. Your life resonates with what is holy and timeless like the sound of a swirling, shaping river. Be open to the love interwoven in that song finding you, changing you, and holding you.*
- *Above all, begin and end with gratitude. This is the well-spring of both a good life and a legacy of kindness. From gratitude comes kindness toward all.*

Calling in the Four Directions

I began this journey across land once home to at least eighteen indigenous tribes by honoring them and honoring my adventure through calling in the four directions. This ritual is commonly associated with Native American/First Nation traditions in North America; its connection to the cardinal directions bears some similarities to traditions in other cultures. The best aspect of this commonality is that it reminds us we are connected universally by the days and seasons of life on this magnificent earth.

The intent of this ritual is to establish spiritual sacredness and set an intention in a physical space. The ritual faces each direction in turn:

- *East: sunrise/spring/childhood/planting/new beginnings*
- *South: midday/summer/youth/tending gardens*
- *West: setting sun/autumn/midlife/harvest*
- *North: winter/night/elderhood/quiet meditation/rest*

When the CDT intersected the Oregon Trail in Wyoming, I considered how my great-great grandparents passed by this place about 170 years earlier. That ground was taken care of by native peoples for centuries. And so, with great reverence, I close this sacred time of sharing stories from the trail and from families' lives by offering a personal interpretation of this ritual.

- *Facing the East: I give thanks for the rising sun, new beginnings each day, open horizons, hopes for each season of life. May you be hopeful.*
- *Facing the South: I give thanks for passion, fire, inspiration, and the warm breath of southern wind that reminds us of summer days and melts the ice that gathers around our hearts. May your heart be open and warm.*
- *Facing the West: I give thanks for the peace that follows the day's effort and offer gratitude for the harvest from a fruitful life. May you be grateful for the prosperity of life well lived.*
- *Facing the North: I give thanks for the gifts of quiet, stillness, and the wisdom and blessings that come to us with time. May your spirit be at peace.*

FOR READER REFLECTION

- *Have there been pivotal experiences in your life that transformed who you are? Who did you become on the other side of those experiences?*

- *What are you most grateful for this week, that gave meaning to your days? After experiencing gratitude, who were you more attentive to?*

- *How would you like your loved ones to remember you?*

- *What are the little moments you share with family and friends that reveal the essence of you as a person and the legacy you want to leave with them?*

A Final Blessing

With a heart full of gratitude for what
the divine has offered on this journey,
for those who helped me to complete it,
for those whose stories I have carried,
for those who have reflected on the waypoints with me,
for ancestors who walked these trails before me,
for those who have tended this land
and the people whose home this land has been,
I give thanks. You have blessed me.

And now, dear reader who has come with me...

Find ways to get in touch with what is good.
Get a good pair of shoes.
Get out there.

ACKNOWLEDGMENTS

I am indebted to countless companions on the trail of events leading to this book.

First, thank you to the families who gave me permission to share their loved ones' stories and excerpts from their memorial services. You became friends, and you will always inspire me.

Thank you to my family members who were my support group on the trail—Bob, Grete, Zach, and Mike—who provided transportation, food, shelter, moral support, gear, advice, first aid, companionship, and rescue. I could never have walked three thousand miles without them at my side, helping from home, or waiting at a trailhead. Special thanks to my husband Bob for listening to my interminable ponderings about gear, hiking logistics, and this book; and for dropping me off or picking me up at too many trailheads to count. Only a champion husband would do that.

Thank you to SCI Funeral Services of Colorado and Denver Market Director Matt Whaley for providing me with the opportunity to help more than four hundred families. I am also particularly grateful for Matt's permission to reconnect with families after my employment so that I could share their stories and honor them additionally in this book. Matt also gave personal attention to my hikes on the CDT, cheering me on each day. I have felt his support throughout my work, my hike, and the development of this book. My gratitude for his confidence in me to take care of families, to complete the CDT, and to write *The Waypoints* is unparalleled.

Thank you to David Wogahn and his team at AuthorImprints for guidance through the waypoints of publishing. Special thanks to Leslie Lehr for developmental edits, and to my copy editor, cover designer, and layout artist.

Thank you to the Celebrant Foundation for my training in celebrating life's transitions—a milestone improvement to my life's path—and to Cherie Karo Schwartz for coaching me in the art of storytelling.

Thank you to those who provided feedback to draft material on my Substack, "Reflections on the Long Walk Home," especially John Marino, Jake Redlawski, Christopher Conroy, and Mike Hull. Thank you to those who read the manuscript and shared their detailed comments—Ben Martin, Susan Gansauer, Jay Brese, Kimra Perkins, Maggie Kneip, Matt Whaley, and Maria Garrod. Your input kept me on a good path.

For providing the maps in this book and guidance in all things CDT, thank you to the Continental Divide Trail Coalition (CDTC), especially Teresa Martinez, executive director, and Zack Bumgarner, GIS specialist.

Thank you to the team of professionals who helped this aging body to keep going and avoid injury—Doctors Sameer Mehta, Katy Mooberry, Abigail Hydock, Weslee Thompson, and Jill Zundelevich; nutritionist and coach Mark Rosenberg; and trainer extraordinaire Susan Wescott, who has kept my body tuned for more than twelve years.

Thank you to angels along the way—especially Kimra Perkins and Randy Sackerson who came to West Yellowstone, Diane Chuprinski in Butte, Tom Wandrych in Helena, Cal Ewing in the Lima Mountains, and Robert Austin and Dan Murphy in the San Juan Mountains.

Thank you to those who hiked more than a couple of miles with me on the CDT—Penelope Purdy, Lisa Shik, Dave Hale, Jann Griffiths, Greg Baker, Matt Anderson, Kathleen Hayden, Zach, Grete, and most of all Mike. Kudos to the animal companions who joined me for a few sections—Blue, Red, and Whalen. You all kept me going.

And finally, thank you to my companion, mentor, patron, and inspiration—dear Francis.

A BONUS STORY

While I was trail angeling April to September 2024 after completing the CDT, I saw the same hikers multiple times along the trail. It was tremendously fun to forge bonds with a handful of people as they proceeded north, connecting with them in New Mexico, Colorado, and Montana.

Me and my trailer in Montana.

My trail angel offerings included food, Gatorade, water, chairs, and most valued of all, transportation. After completing a trail section, hikers needed to get into town to resupply their food. Near the end of the trail, hikers also needed to pick up backcountry permits to pass through Glacier National Park and cross the border into Canada.

Amy was one of those I aided more than once on her trek north.

I first met Amy in a tiny hiker-friendly town devoted to a dessert: Pie Town, New Mexico. She had taken time off from her job in Canada to hike the CDT beginning to end, some of it solo and some with hikers she met along the way.

I assisted her in New Mexico in April as she was beginning; we re-connected in Colorado in June when a forest fire closed part of the trail. For five days, I picked up hikers scrambling to get around the fire and back on the trail north of Leadville. I drove Amy to the store that had her supply box, and then to the next trailhead so she could keep hiking. Then we stayed in touch over the summer as she continued north.

Planning to trail angel in northern Montana around the time Amy would complete the CDT, I began to think it would be fun to see her at the trail's end. That would complete my staying in touch with her from start to finish.

Lo and behold, in the first week of September, I dashed down the trail from Waterton, Canada, and arrived at the US/Canada border monument to join Amy's mother *ten minutes* before Amy walked up the trail and into her mom's welcoming arms. What a gift to be included in celebrating Amy's completion of the CDT!

Our little celebration at the border ended my trail angel season on a high note. I was reminded how satisfying it is to support good people in achieving their goals. They did the hard work; I was in the cheering section. Assisting hikers energized my entry into a new chapter in life—retired from full-time employment and very long hikes, but still engaged and contributing.

By the time I completed the CDT, accompanying grieving families had quieted me and given me a new connection to *life*: They broke open my heart to a gentle grace. On the trail and on the journey of grief, I learned to be present to the people who come down the path. We are all capable of growing angel wings.

Amy and me at the border.

DISCUSSION QUESTIONS

I f you have read this book as part of a book club, your discussion leader might want to look back at the Reader Reflection questions at the end of each Waypoint and select one for each topic. This would provide ten questions for a comprehensive discussion of the book.

As an alternative, the questions offered for Reader Reflection at the end of Waypoint 10, *Reaching the Summit*, could be used on their own to lead a discussion. Try to consider these questions in advance. Responses will provide poignant insights into each person's life experiences and how you and your friends hope to be remembered.

This may not appeal to every age group, but if everyone in your club is open to this, consider a roundtable sharing of what each person hopes their memorial service will be like. This isn't morbid; it's practical and very helpful to the people who care about you. I assure you that many light-hearted memories will surface. Here are some ideas for envisioning an experience that, when you're not here to express your opinion, will authentically capture who you were:

- *Looking back on what you love doing, what would a perfect day in your life include? What stories are connected to your best times? These should be lovingly captured in memories of you.*

- *What mementos could represent your interests and what you love?*

- *What has been particularly important to you in living your life? What have been the guiding values that you hope your family and friends will carry forward?*

- *What made you laugh? What are a few particularly funny memories?*

- *What are your favorite songs or pieces of music?*

- *Do you have spiritual beliefs that should be acknowledged when people gather to remember your life?*

- *Is there anything else that you hope the gathering will include? Do you have a suggestion for a gathering place meaningful to you?*

- *Are there words you would like someone to read to your family and friends?*

- *Have you written down your wishes and shared them with your family? (Information on what you want is a gift to your family, so they won't be left wondering what to do when the time comes.)*

- *We're glad you're with us! Is there something that your life hasn't included yet that is still possible and that you hope you will experience?*

Depending on the size of your group, it could take a while to work through this. Consider spreading these discussions over more than one meeting. Afterwards, you will have a deeper understanding of your friends' hopes for their life and legacy. Use what you learn as an opportunity to affirm the hopes of the people in your circle. How can you support each other? New insights might even shape your choices for future reading.

When you help each other bloom, you will be a well-spring of grace to people you care about.

REFERENCES

Bakos, Lisa M. "Farewell Prayer." Hoofbeats In Heaven. 2023. Accessed December 11, 2024. https://hoofbeats-in-heaven.com/praise/A-L/Farewell_Prayer/.

Bolz-Weber, Nadia. "You're going to die." The Corners. November 6, 2023. Accessed December 11, 2024. https://thecorners.substack.com/p/youre-going-to-die.

Gansauer, Diane. "Crossing the River." *Deep Wild Journal*, no. 4 (2022): 31-43. Accessed December 11, 2024. https://deepwild-journal.com/wp-content/uploads/2023/10/dw4-master-book-to-print-06-20-2022-final.pdf.

Gansauer, Diane. "Good Choices." *Deep Wild Journal*, no. 2 (2020): 60-63. Accessed December 11, 2024. https://deepwildjournal.com/wp-content/uploads/2021/07/dw2-master-book-vol-2-july-4-2020.pdf.

King Jr, Neil. *American Ramble: A Walk of Memory and Renewal.* Mariner Books, 2023.

Riley, Cole Arthur. *This Here Flesh: Spirituality, Liberation, and the Stories That Make Us.* Convergent Books, 2022. Excerpt(s) and "Chapter Three: Wonder" used by permission of Convergent Books, an imprint of Random House, a division of Penguin Random House LLC. All rights reserved.

Rohr, Richard. *Just This.* CAC Publishing, 2007. Cited by permission of CAC Publishing. All rights reserved worldwide.

Wohlleben, Peter. *The Hidden Life of Trees: What They Feel, How They Communicate—Discoveries from a Secret World.* Greystone Books, 2016.

York, Trisha C. "Down This River." 2016. Unpublished. Used by permission of the poet. All rights reserved.

PHOTO CREDITS

Front cover: The author

Title page: Lisa Shik.

Introduction: Zachary Miller.

Waypoint 2: Group photo by Kimra Perkins.

Waypoint 5: The wild horses and pronghorn photos in the Great Divide Basin taken by CDT hiker Steve Hawks.

Waypoint 7: Photo of author and daughter at a cairn by Zachary Miller. Photo of author and her brother entering Yellowstone by Kimra Perkins.

Waypoint 9: Photo of author and brother crossing the river by Zachary Miller.

Waypoint 10: Photo at the northern border monument by Zachary Miller. Photo of the jump into Waterton Lake by Grete Gansauer. Cairn photo by Steve Hawks.

Acknowledgments: Zachary Miller.

Bonus story: Photo of Amy and author by Amy's mother.

Back cover: Lisa Shik.

All other trail photos were taken by the author, her brother, or a stranger using the author's phone.

ILLUSTRATIONS

All maps were provided by the Continental Divide Trail Coalition. Compiled from public data available through CGIAR, Esri, FAO, Garmin, the GIS User Community, OAA, OpenStreetMap contributors, and TomTom.

RESOURCES

Exploring the Continental Divide Trail (CDT):

The Continental Divide Trail Coalition (CDTC) is the 501(c)(3) national non-profit working in partnership with the US Forest Service, National Park Service, and Bureau of Land Management to complete, promote, and protect the Continental Divide National Scenic Trail. Founded in 2012 by a passionate group of volunteers and recreationists, CDTC is a membership organization working to build a strong community of supporters who want to see the CDT protected not just for today's users, but for generations to come. You can start exploring the trail by using CDTC's interactive map and other resources on their website. https://cdtcoalition.org/

Celebrant training and finding a Celebrant:

The Natural Transitions Institute (NTI) offers training for purpose-driven individuals from all walks of life a way to serve others through heart-centered and transformational ceremonies marking life's milestones. The author was on the faculty of North America's first accredited celebrancy training institute, the Celebrant Foundation and Institute, whose course materials passed to NTI when it opened in 2025.

NTI also offers a convenient map of celebrants in your area with their Find a Celebrant application. https://www.naturaltransitions.org/

Recognizing the value of ceremony professionals in honoring lives, a growing number of funeral providers can connect families directly to funeral celebrants. An independent celebrant is also an option.

ABOUT THE AUTHOR

There is a custom on long distance trails to use a trail name rather than your usual name. You aren't supposed to give yourself your own trail name; it must be given to you, typically by other hikers and often when they see you do something weird or stupid. When Diane was given the trail name "Grace" by a good friend, she snapped it up immediately before someone could give her a name for doing something weird or stupid. She likes the name Grace because it helps her aspire to being her best self.

Diane writes about the milestones and transitions in life, distilled through her experience as a long-distance hiker and as the officiant for more than four hundred funerals and a few hundred other ceremonies honoring transitions in life. She is also a trail angel to other hikers on their long treks and she continues to hike extensively—although not three thousand miles at a time anymore.

Trailer and trail name with the figure of Francis of Assisi, a reminder to be gracious.

Celebrant work appeals to her creative side and her desire to help people. It also gave her a break from a long administrative career in wildlife and land conservation that had become increasingly technical and politically stressful. Diane's positions included executive director of Colorado Wildlife Federation and deputy director of Great Outdoors Colorado.

She began to look for a creative outlet, tending to a side of her life that she hadn't paid attention to since she was a performing arts and visual arts major in college, where she especially enjoyed choreography. Intrigued with the role of ceremonies in marking life transitions, she turned to celebrant training in 2011.

Celebrants are schooled in the art of ritual, ceremony, world traditions, faith traditions, mythology, ceremonial writing, and public speaking. They can officiate at virtually every life event with a focus on personalizing each ceremony to reflect the needs, beliefs, and values of the couple or family. Diane loves working with people to make something beautiful, spiritually rich, and uplifting.

Diane has been telling life stories as a means of honoring the essence of individuals and the sacredness of life transitions since becoming certified as a Life-Cycle Celebrant in 2012 by the Celebrant Foundation and Institute. She went on to earn recognition as a Master Celebrant and subsequently joined the Celebrant Foundation's faculty.

Diane's background also includes a doctorate in ministry from The New Seminary, the country's oldest interfaith seminary. She embraced interfaith studies to be of better service to people of all spiritual perspectives, including those who are agnostic.

Diane initiated the Funeral Celebrant program at a group of funeral homes in metro-Denver; they honored her with a Lifetime Achievement Award in 2021.

She now provides ceremonies through her company Lyrical Life Ceremonies (www.LyricalLifeCeremonies.com) and publishes through Lyrical Life Press.

Essays by Diane have been published in *Deep Wild: Writing from the Backcountry,* the CDT Coalition's magazine *Passages,* the magazine of the Funeral Directors Association, and the handbook *Life Cycle Ceremonies* published by the Celebrant Foundation.

Diane lives in Evergreen, Colorado, with her husband Bob. They have been married more than forty years and raised daughter Grete, who raises her parents to higher levels all the time.

Diane can be contacted through her website
LyricalLifeCeremonies.com
and by email at
CeremoniesDiane@gmail.com.

She is available for public speaking.